Helping Students Write to a Prompt

by Sydell Rabin

SCHOLASTIC
PROFESSIONALBOOKS

NEW YORK • TORONTO • LONDON • AUCKLAND • SYDNEY
MEXICO CITY • NEW DELHI • HONG KONG • BUENOS AIRES

Acknowledgements

As a teacher and department head of English in South Orange and Maplewood, New Jersey, I have learned from my students and my colleagues, from Janet Emig and James Moffett, Lucy Calkins, Nancie Atwell, Peter Elbow, Donald Graves, and Donald Murray. And I've learned from my husband, Arnold, who is himself a writer.

I want to thank the many teachers who helped me in this project by sharing their students' work with me. Thank you so much, Jane Muratti and Lucille Levy from Passaic, Sandy Boutsikaris and Laura Fenn from Westfield, Jennie Paul and Kelly Pedersen from the Kushner Academy, and Ryan O'Dell, Paula Appenzoller, and Diana Hill from Maplewood/South Orange, and Joanna Davis-Swing, my editor, for her enthusiasm and good advice.

Cover design by Norma Ortiz
Cover photo by Vicky Kasala
Interior design by Sarah Morrow

Copyright © 2002 by Sydell Rabin
All rights reserved. Published by Scholastic Inc.
Printed in the U.S.A.
ISBN 0-439-29641-2

1 2 3 4 5 6 7 8 9 10   40   09 08 07 06 05 04 03 02

Table of Contents

Introduction

Most students have only the vaguest notion of what constitutes good writing. And neither grammar books stressing correctness nor collections with model essays by Charles Lamb or Ernest Hemingway will teach them how to write. In my experience, the best way to help students improve their writing skills is to involve them in the evaluation process. A few years ago, in an effort to prepare my students for upcoming state assessments, I did just that—and the results were astounding. My students learned and internalized the language that experienced writers and teachers use to discuss the craft of writing, and this gave them invaluable insight into what makes good writing good. In this book, I will share the results of that experience, along with all of the tools you'll need to implement it in your classroom.

Helping Students Write to a Prompt contains a series of classroom lessons using student-writing models to teach kids how to evaluate writing. The lessons put students in the teacher's chair for a moment, asking them to read and to score a variety of essays. By taking on the role of evaluator—a role generally reserved for the teacher—students learn the teacher's vocabulary and criteria, and begin to understand what they must do in their own writing so that their ideas and feelings can reach their readers clearly and effectively. The teacher-guided discussion that follows each scoring session focuses students' attention on the writing elements you want to teach. Students will also write their own essays and learn to evaluate them with the same critical eye they've been applying to the samples.

The six essay topics included in this book are representative of writing topics middle-school students are typically assigned, both for in-class work and writing assessments. Each topic is followed by four writing samples, ranging in quality from a "4" (a very well-developed and well-written sample) to a "1" (a poorly developed paper, flawed with errors of usage and mechanics). The models are based on composites of student writing collected over a period of years from many different student populations. Because I believe that the whole is better than the sum of its parts, I use the holistic scoring approach—in which readers assign a number score based on their response to the essay as a whole—instead of dissecting a paper. Most state assessments are also scored holistically, and I want to emphasize the development of ideas and content rather than the hunt for errors. Although I use a four-point scale in these lessons for instructional purposes, teachers who wish to use a six-point scale (the scale used in most state testing) can refer to the Appendix for additional papers and directions. The discussion prompts that follow each essay can serve as a jumping-off point to a class discussion of writing techniques, which further enhances students' understanding of the qualities of good writing.

The first section of the book introduces the rubric, checklist, and response sheet students use when evaluating writing. I also discuss holistic evaluation and the writing behaviors of middle-school students. Then I present a series of lessons incorporating these tools and ideas. The lessons help students identify what constitutes good writing and give them practice applying their criteria to pieces of writing.

The second section of the book contains the writing prompts, model student essays, and discussion prompts for each essay. Finally, the Appendix contains a six-point rubric and additional essays for those who wish to use the six-point scale with their students.

There is no magic formula to help students become writers but some methods are better than others. I know that I learned all about commas when I had to teach them; and that when I recognized my own writing problems in other people's writing, I understood why I needed to edit my own work carefully. Moreover, when I saw the risks other writers were willing to take, I was emboldened to take some of my own.

I hope that what distinguishes this text from others is that I ask students to deal with whole papers, with realistic expectations at each grade level, with grammar taught in context, and with an opportunity to role-play the teacher.

Sydell Rabin

Chapter 1

Laying the Groundwork

Helping Students Identify the Elements of Good Writing

Students become stronger writers by reading and evaluating the writing of others. The first step is for students to understand and recognize the qualities that make good writing. Then students can begin to write essays that contain those qualities. The rubrics, checklist, and lessons presented in this chapter help students accomplish these goals.

Using a Rubric

A rubric is an excellent way to illustrate the elements of good writing, and it serves as a reference point for both students and teachers as they evaluate a piece of writing. I've developed a master rubric that divides the characteristics of good writing into four broad categories that reflect the divisions used by many state assessments: *content and organization*, *sentence construction*, *usage*, and *mechanics*. Within each category is a set of criteria that describes the features of good writing. These criteria are easily translated into the writing skills that middle-grade students need to acquire. But before we can help students identify and discuss good writing, we must first introduce students to the idea that there are specific qualities of good writing and teach them the vocabulary to describe those qualities. Rubrics are an effective tool here as well.

Following is a description of the characteristics I've placed in each category. You'll find the master rubric on page 9 and a simplified version for student use on page 18. I often share the master rubric with students and base my evaluations of their work on it. However, I've found the simplified version easier for students to use when they are evaluating writing, and I've ensured it contains the same categories and vocabulary as the master rubric.

What Makes Good Writing Good: Some Characteristics

Content/Organization

1. The content creates an effective and well-developed response to the prompt.

2. The paper has many related ideas, supported with mature reasoning, examples, details, or facts.

3. The paper is organized with an introduction, a middle section that develops the ideas, and a satisfying conclusion based on the ideas presented in the paper.

4. The writer understands how to use paragraphs, developing each new point fully in a unified paragraph.

5. There's a logical sequence to the ideas.

6. The writer understands how to use transitional devices or linking words and phrases.

7. The content is well thought-out, interesting, and carries the honest sound of the writer's voice.

8. Fictional and narrative writing make their own demands but still require focused content with appropriate description, development of character, narrative details, and paragraphing consistent with direct and indirect discourse.

9. The writer understands the purpose of the essay and the audience for whom it is intended.

Sentence Construction

1. The writer has a strong command of sentence structure and does not write in fragments or run-on sentences.

2. Sentences are appropriately varied. The writer knows how to use compound and complex structures, demonstrating the ability to combine related ideas in dependent clauses and prepositional phrases.

3. The writer uses parallel structure to unite related ideas.

4. The writer avoids unnecessary shifts from one subject to another. The writer also avoids unnecessary shifts in verb tense.

5. The writer knows how to write, punctuate, and paragraph dialogue correctly.

6. The writer places modifiers correctly so that the meaning of the sentence is clear.

Usage

1. The writer uses language appropriate for the audience and the occasion.
2. The writer understands the basics of grammar and makes few errors in subject-verb agreement, pronoun reference, pronoun case, verb form, adjective agreement, correct use of idioms, and correct use of adjectives and adverbs. (Additional usage concerns may be added to this list as the class learns more concepts.)
3. The writer avoids indefinite-pronoun references.
4. The writer can distinguish between homonyms. (Homonym errors are included in this category as separate from spelling errors.)

Mechanics

1. The writer follows spelling conventions.
2. The writer understands the rules of capitalization.
3. The writer knows how to use commas and apostrophes and is learning to use other internal marks of punctuation like semicolons, colons, dashes, and parentheses, not only to clarify but to enhance meaning.

The categories are all teacher terms, the rules by which we read and evaluate papers and the rules by which official graders assess state writing tests. Except for spelling and punctuation, most students have not internalized these criteria. The process of internalizing them takes time and patience as well as the focused feedback of a teacher who always uses the same vocabulary to explain his or her response to a piece of writing. Using a rubric helps maintain that consistency of response throughout the year.

For instructional purposes, I use a four-point scale, but if you wish to use the six-point scale many state assessments employ, you will find additional essays and a six-point rubric in the Appendix.

Using the Master Rubric

As you evaluate essays, you can use the master rubric to keep you focused on these categories and on the possible skill level demonstrated in the paper.

Master Rubric

Score 4	Score 3	Score 2	Score 1
The writer has a strong control of written language.	*The writer has a good command of written language.*	*This paper reveals limited skill in written expression.*	*The writer lacks control of written expression.*

Content/Organization

Score 4	Score 3	Score 2	Score 1
• Is organized effectively around a single focus. • Includes appropriate details, examples, and reasons • Moves logically from opening to closing • Demonstrates analytical, critical, and/or creative thinking. • Contains interesting and original ideas • Contains unified, well-developed paragraphs with transitions between ideas	• Is organized effectively • Develops one idea in each paragraph • Includes some details, examples, or reasons • Leaves room for further development of ideas	• Attempts to develop main ideas, but paragraphs do not have enough details, examples, or reasons • Does not stick to one idea per paragraph • Separates ideas that go together into different paragraphs • Lacks transitions between ideas and paragraphs	• Does not develop a main idea • Lacks a beginning, a middle, or an ending • Does not use paragraphs • Does not communicate purpose clearly

Sentence Construction

Score 4	Score 3	Score 2	Score 1
• Uses a variety of sentence structures effectively • Contains few, if any, errors in sentence construction • Uses sophisticated devices (such as dependent clauses, appositives, and parallel structure) to show relationships between ideas	• Contains some errors in sentence construction	• Lacks sentence variety • Contains syntactical errors, such as shifts in simple subjects, dangling modifiers, run-ons, and fragments	• Contains frequent syntactical errors • Contains incoherent sentences, sometimes because important connecting words are missing or incorrectly used • Includes short, choppy sentences and/or long, rambling ones

Usage

Score 4	Score 3	Score 2	Score 1
• Contains few, if any, errors in grammar • Uses appropriate language for audience and purpose of piece	• Shows an awareness of audience and purpose • Demonstrates a good command of language, although some errors in grammar appear, usually with pronouns	• Contains frequent grammar errors, especially with pronoun agreement and pronoun reference. • Includes inexact or inappropriate word choice	• Contains significant usage problems, such as subject-verb agreement, pronoun use, and word choice • Includes inappropriate word choice

Mechanics

Score 4	Score 3	Score 2	Score 1
• Includes few, if any, errors in mechanics	• Contains relatively few errors in spelling, capitalization and punctuation	• Contains mistakes in spelling and punctuation that don't interfere with reading.	• Includes many mechanical errors that interfere with the reader's understanding

Scoring Holistically

Using a rubric and scoring holistically will help you give students specific feedback in a timely fashion that is targeted to their needs. It also helps students focus on the big picture instead of getting caught up in the details of a piece. When you evaluate a piece of writing holistically, you consider the piece as a whole and assign it a rank based on the criteria laid out in the rubric. You highlight specific areas that you want students to focus on without marking every single error. You can choose beforehand to look only for issues related to, say, content and organization, or you may decide to address one or two issues that clearly need to be brought to the writer's attention.

Before beginning to score a group of papers holistically, it's important to note the following ideas:

- Read all papers in a set before scoring any one of them. You are not trying to establish an absolute standard but to compare the quality of first-draft papers written during a class period.

- Remember that scoring papers is not an exact science and there is healthy room for disagreement. To best help the writer, always show them an example of what you mean.

- Keep it in mind that the best papers aren't perfect and the poorest papers can still have worthwhile ideas.

Asking students to score one another's papers holistically makes the evaluation process more manageable for them. I give them a rubric (either the master rubric or the student version) and a checklist (see page 19) to guide their evaluation, always reminding them that they don't have to agree on every point. One of the most important goals in asking students to read, examine, and score one another's papers is the interaction between students and teacher as student writers begin to understand the vocabulary of evaluation.

The Role of the Teacher

Some of you may be tempted to ask, "So what is the teacher's role in this process?" Rest assured, you are not turning over instruction to your students. A critical part of this model of teaching writing is the guidance of the teacher as the class comes together to discuss the student-written papers. The class discussion is a prime teaching opportunity, where you can choose issues your students need to address in their own work and lead the discussion to those issues, using the essays as examples of the characteristic you want students to focus on. Is the class as a whole having trouble choosing vivid verbs? Ask them to look closely at the choice of verbs in the weakest and strongest papers and share what they notice. Are the majority of students relying on lead questions to open their pieces? Choose a set of papers that demonstrates other techniques and invite students to analyze these leads, encouraging them to discuss what works and what doesn't—and to add the approaches that work to their own repertoire. Holistic evaluation is an excellent way to target writing instruction that fits your students' specific needs.

To help you get the most out of student-written essays and papers, I've provided discussion prompts that will help you guide the discussion in productive ways. (See "Teacher's Guide," page 46 and on, for each prompt and sample essay.)

Writing Behaviors in the Middle Years

Writing develops in a classroom where it is viewed as an essential means of communication, where writers get a chance to practice writing in a variety of forms for different audiences and different purposes. If we give young writers multiple opportunities to write, they will acquire the following behaviors and skills. This list of writing behaviors has been adapted from the "Report on Writing" by the National Education Assessment Program (NEAP) for grades 4 through 8.

- Students know there are stages to writing—drafting, revising, editing, and proofreading.
- Students can add information to earlier drafts.
- Students respond to the writing of peers in small groups.
- Students are learning to view their own and others' works critically.
- Students are developing editing and proofreading skills, including editing for word choice and expanding sentence patterns.
- Students can proofread individually and collaboratively for conventional usage: spelling, capitalization, and punctuation.
- Students apply appropriate conventions for dialogue, quotations, and letters.
- As they mature, students are able to explain and demonstrate how written communication is affected by language, tone, and voice.
- Students develop a sense of personal voice or style that varies with audience and purpose.
- Students can use the mechanics of writing to clarify meaning.

The holistic evaluation process in this book will help students master these behaviors and skills. As they learn how to evaluate the writing of other students, they will also learn how to write more effectively themselves. The continual interwoven process of writing and responding to papers helps students internalize the features of strong writing. This process moves along an upward spiral as students understand the traits of effective writing on higher, more sophisticated levels and become more able to apply those traits to their own work.

Getting Started With Holistic Grading

With all this in mind—what constitutes good writing and what middle-school students need to learn about the writing process—I've developed a series of lessons to help students discover for themselves the qualities of good writing and apply their thoughts as they evaluate sample essays:

These lessons provide the groundwork for students to evaluate papers critically—those of others and eventually their own. The awareness of the qualities of good writing that such evaluation provides improves students' work immensely.

Lesson 1: Identifying the Qualities of Good Writing

Inviting students to participate in a discussion of what makes good writing helps establish a collaborative learning environment and is very motivating for middle-schoolers. It helps them feel invested in the evaluation process and gives them a sense of control over their writing. The following lesson guides students to articulate the qualities of strong writing discussed earlier. The ideas come from the students, but your careful guidance can elicit clarifications, focus students on key ideas, and group their criteria for good writing in appropriate categories. The lesson might go something like this:

Mrs. R.: I have an idea for your next paper, but before you write, I'd like all of us to talk about writing: What makes writing "good"? And who's to say whether it is good or not—the writer or the reader? As writers, it's important for us to realize that writing is only one side of the coin. On the other side is reading. So, in this next lesson, I want you to be a good reader as well as a good writer. Until now, I've been the only one who has graded your writing or made helpful comments on it. Now you're going to learn how to be a good reader and how to make helpful comments to a writer. There's a double advantage to this. By helping someone else write better, you're going to discover that you are becoming a better writer, too. Let's start by making a list of the characteristics of good writing. Tell me what you think.

Jerri: It's got to be interesting.

Mrs. R.: (writes the word on the board with a dash after it) What do you mean by "interesting"?

Jerri: Something that catches your attention.

Travis: Something that makes sense.

Allyson: It tells you something that makes you laugh, or you learn something.

Jenny: The writer has good ideas.

Mrs. R.: (writes these on the board, abbreviating as necessary) Good. I'm so glad you talked about ideas first. What else makes writing easy and enjoyable for the reader?

Latisha: The writer uses paragraphs.

Sam: Sentences with correct punctuation.

Andy: No run-on sentences.

Sally: The beginning should make you want to read more.

Brian: And the last paragraph should be interesting.

Mrs. R.: There's that word again. What do you mean by "interesting"?

Brian: I don't know—it should make you think more about what the writer said, or it could be a summary, a conclusion. But it should be interesting.

Mrs. R.: Good enough. I get the point. What else can a writer do to make the reader happy?

Latisha: Use colorful words. A good vocabulary.

Mrs. R.: Is there anything that makes a reader unhappy?

Latisha: Bad grammar and spelling.

Sam: When there's no punctuation, so you can't tell when a new sentence starts.

Cathy: Boring sentences.

Mrs. R.: Wonderful. You've given me a good working list of writing problems that could certainly turn a reader away. We have to do something else now. Looking at this list, we can see that some problems go together and are different from others. I mean, having "good ideas" is not the same as "knowing how to spell giraffe." Let's divide the list into categories of things that go together. Take a few minutes to think on paper and tell me which characteristics you would group together and why. Use numbers to group like items together. (*after two or three minutes*) How should we divide the list? Let's put a number next to all the ideas that go together, and then we'll give each group a heading.

Latisha: I would put a "1" next to all the answers that are about ideas and having a good opening and ending.

Mrs. R.: Very good. Those points are all about the content of the paper and how it's put together or organized. (*writes "Content/Organization" on the board, circles content-related items on the list, and draws arrows connecting them to the heading*) What's another category?

Eric: Spelling and punctuation, bad grammar.

Mrs. R.: Yes. But I'd like to separate bad grammar from spelling and punctuation because using the wrong word is not really the same as misspelling it. Let's call "spelling" and "punctuation" the "mechanics" of writing because they are the technical part of writing, the part that makes the writing easy to read. You have to do the writing first—ideas, sentences, paragraphs—before you pay attention to spelling and commas. (*writes "Mechanics" as a heading but leaves space between it and the Content/Organization heading; circles the words "spelling" and "punctuation" on the list and draws arrows to the heading*)

Cathy: Is "Sentences" a category?

Mrs. R.: Yes, I think that's a good one because the ideas have to be written in sentences. Let's make "Sentence Construction" our second heading. (*writes Sentence Construction on the board, circles "no run-ons" and "boring sentences," and draws arrows from them to the heading*) Now, tell me, where would you put "paragraphs"?

Allyson: With Content.

Mrs. R.: Why?

Allyson: Because ideas get developed in paragraphs.

Mrs. R.: …and that makes up the content. Good. We still have items floating on the list. Can we group them under a heading?

Sam: Vocabulary. Colorful words.

Mrs. R.: Yes, the words we use make another category. (*writes "Usage" on the board, circles that item on the list and draws an arrow to the heading*) Where would you put mistakes in grammar like "more better," or "I want them cookies"? Or "there" instead of "their"?

Eddie: Mechanics? Because it's a mistake?

Mrs. R.: But is it a mistake like a spelling mistake? (*allows for a discussion of the most suitable category for grammar errors until students realize that grammar errors are word choices that belong under Usage*)

Before we go ahead, let's think of a few more characteristics of good writing and see which heading we would use for them.

Latisha: Paragraphs should stick to one point.

Mrs. R.: And the heading?

Latisha: Content.

Mrs. R.: Excellent. Now one more.

Harry: Ideas should flow. I'm not sure whether that's Sentence Construction or Content.

Mrs. R.: You're talking about ideas and how one logically follows another. What do you think?

Harry: I think it's Content because it's about more than one sentence.

Mrs. R.: Great. Now let's collect all of this information so we'll remember it. On a clean page in your notebooks, write Content/Organization and list those characteristics. Do the same for Sentence Construction, Usage, and Mechanics.

Lesson 2: Developing a Writing Checklist

Once students have determined the basic categories for evaluating writing (see Lesson 1), the next step is to create a checklist from the information to help students identify those traits in a specific piece of writing. Although I have provided a ready-to-use checklist based on a composite of those created by past classes, inviting your students to develop their own checklist based on their discussion is an excellent learning experience. The checklist I include is based on the master rubric on page 9. You may choose to share the rubric with your students at this point, explaining that it captures the qualities of good writing, that it's often used as an assessment tool for the state tests, and that you'll be using it to evaluate their essays. I have found that the checklist format is useful for students, especially at first. Students can then use their responses on the checklist to give an essay a score from the rubric. I've also developed a student-friendly rubric (see page 18).

To develop a checklist with your class, select a paper from another class or another year to evaluate together. Make enough copies for everyone. I would begin the lesson like this:

Writing Checklist for Students

	Yes	Generally	Sometimes	No
Content/Organization				
Does the opening make a reader want to read more?				
Is the conclusion logical and satisfying?				
Does the writer give us interesting ideas?				
Are the ideas fully developed with reasons and examples?				
Is it easy to follow the ideas from one sentence to the next, from one paragraph to the next?				
Does the writer stick to the point?				
Is the writer's voice clear, strong, and honest?				
Sentence Construction				
Is each sentence complete?				
Is it easy to follow the meaning of each sentence?				
Does the writer use a variety of sentences and know how to combine ideas that go together in phrases and clauses?				
If the writer uses dialogue, is it punctuated and indented correctly?				
Usage				
Is the language effective and appropriate for the occasion and audience?				
Does the writer use correct grammar, making few errors, especially with pronouns and verb tense?				
If homonyms are used, has the writer chosen the correct ones?				
Has the writer avoided wordiness?				
Mechanics				
Are the words spelled correctly?				
Are the words correctly capitalized?				
Does the writer punctuate sentences correctly?				

Mrs. R.: I think we said some very important things yesterday about writing. Let's take another look at the ideas we generated, see what else we can add, and then put them all to work as a checklist as we evaluate a sample paper. What do we have so far under the first heading, Content/Organization?

Sally: The writing has good ideas. A good opening and conclusion.

Mrs. R: *(after Sally has finished)* Is there anything else that we could add? *(agrees with students on what should be added, and then proceeds through each of the other categories; explains this doesn't have to be exhaustive and should take no more than 15 minutes)* Now we have a workable checklist, something you will be able to use almost like a ruler to see how a paper measures up to your expectations. Put a checkmark in the column that best describes whether the paper does what the question asks. Put a check under "Yes" if it does so regularly. Put a check under "Generally" if it does so most of the time but not always. Put a check under "Sometimes" if the writer does it once or twice. Put a check under "No" if the writer doesn't do it at all.

Here is an essay I'd like you to read. *(allows a few minutes while students read the paper)* Now let's look at the checklist under Content/Organization. I want you to pick three items under that heading and see if the paper you've just read does any of those things or has any of those qualities. *(calls on three or four students and allows time for the class to discuss whether the items do indeed apply to the paper)* Very good work. Let's do the same thing with the next category, Sentence Construction. *(takes the class through each category, seeing how the items relate to the paper they have all just read)*

Lesson 3: Using the Checklist to Evaluate Sample Essays Holistically

To prepare for this lesson in which students will practice scoring papers on their own, you'll need to select and duplicate a set of four typical compositions. Each student will need to work on his or her own set. The papers can be drawn from last year's classes or borrowed from a colleague. Also, students will need to know the original prompt to which the sample essays are responding.

Preparing Practice Papers

The practice set of papers should:
- represent a range of ability from 4 (the best) to 1 (the weakest)
- be identified by a fictitious name, a letter, or a number
- all be on the same topic

For this lesson, you'll need to prepare:

- a set of four papers for each student (from your own files or borrowed from a colleague)
- four response sheets for each student (see page 20)
- one Writing Checklist for each student (see page 19)
- one Holistic Scoring Guide for each student (see page 18)

Before students read the practice set of papers, give them each a copy of the Holistic Scoring Guide (see page 18). Read the page aloud with them, emphasizing that students should consider the papers as a whole and not get bogged down in details. Remind them to read all the papers before assigning any scores, and encourage them to be respectful in their comments. The Holistic Scoring Guide includes a simplified four-point rubric for students.

On the board, chart paper, or an overhead, copy the sample Response Sheet (see page 20)—or distribute copies—and ask students to use a Response Sheet to record their comments for each paper. (Each student will need four response sheets—one for each essay.)

Now they're ready to read the set of four practice papers you have prepared. Distribute the papers and allow 20 to 30 minutes for students to read them. Ask students not to talk to their neighbors while they're reading and responding; they will have plenty of time the next day to share their responses. If students have questions, you can help them, but be careful not to suggest a response. At the end of the period, have students put their work in their classroom folders.

Holistic Scoring Guide

Before beginning to score papers, follow these rules:

1. Read all papers in the set before scoring any one of them.

2. Remember that the best papers aren't necessarily perfect, and the weakest papers can still make good points.

3. Read the whole paper before you score it. Here are some guidelines to help you decide on the score. You also have a Response Sheet for recording your score and explaining it.

Score 4 This is the best paper in the set as far as content and organization are concerned. The writer has few, if any, problems with sentences. Vocabulary is good, and there are very few, if any, problems with grammar or mechanics. "Yes" will be the response to almost all of the questions on your checklist.

Score 3 This is also a good paper. The content holds your interest, and the paper is well organized. It has a beginning, a middle, and a conclusion. Some of the ideas may need further development, but basically, the paper is well written with few errors in grammar or mechanics.

Score 2 This paper may have good ideas, but they are not well developed. The paragraphs are skimpy. Sometimes the paragraphs are repetitious. Sentences often lack variety and may be difficult to understand. There may also be errors in grammar and mechanics.

Score 1 This paper has serious writing problems. There isn't very much content, and what content is there has not been developed. There usually isn't an opening or a conclusion. There are several sentence errors like run-ons and fragments, as well as mistakes in grammar, vocabulary, and mechanics. On your checklist, you will probably answer "no" most often.

Writing Checklist for Students

	Yes	Generally	Sometimes	No
Content/Organization				
Does the opening make a reader want to read more?				
Is the conclusion logical and satisfying?				
Does the writer give us interesting ideas?				
Are the ideas fully developed with reasons and examples?				
Is it easy to follow the ideas from one sentence to the next, from one paragraph to the next?				
Does the writer stick to the point?				
Is the writer's voice clear, strong, and honest?				
Sentence Construction				
Is each sentence complete?				
Is it easy to follow the meaning of each sentence?				
Does the writer use a variety of sentences and know how to combine ideas that go together in phrases and clauses?				
If the writer uses dialogue, is it punctuated and indented correctly?				
Usage				
Is the language effective and appropriate for the occasion and audience?				
Does the writer use correct grammar, making few errors, especially with pronouns and verb tense?				
If homonyms are used, has the writer chosen the correct ones?				
Has the writer avoided wordiness?				
Mechanics				
Are the words spelled correctly?				
Are the words correctly capitalized?				
Does the writer punctuate sentences correctly?				

Response Sheet

1. What is the code/name of the paper you are scoring? _____

2. Your score is [　] .

3. Using your Writing Checklist and Holistic Scoring Guide as references, explain how you scored this paper and why. Give one or two examples of the parts you think are good and those you think are weak or incorrect.

Content/Organization

Sentence Construction

Usage

Mechanics

Tallying Results and Sharing Responses From Lesson 3

Have students take out the previous day's work on rating essays from their folders. Today you will want them to share the results of yesterday's scoring (on the four-point scale) and discuss their responses, even if everyone wasn't able to finish. You might start the discussion by drawing a chart on the board to record their scores.

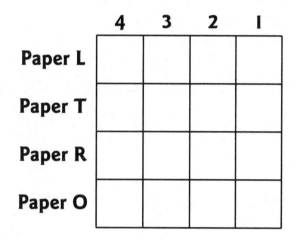

Mrs. R.:   Let's take out yesterday's work and see what scores you gave the essays. I'm going to make a chart on the board with the letter code of each essay on one side and the points scored on the other.

           How many of you gave essay L a 4? a 3? a 2? a 1? *(tallies the scores)*

Note: If the practice papers selected contain reasonable and significant differences among them, the results will be predictable. Most students will be able to separate the better papers from the weaker ones.

Mrs. R.:   Now, let's look at this. Most of us seem to agree that L is the best paper in the set. O is a close second. And T and R follow in that order. *(focuses first on the better papers)* Those of you who chose L, tell us why. Use your Response Sheet and Writing Checklist to explain your answers.

Eric: I think the content of L has more to it that O. I gave O a 3 because it's good, but not as good as L.

Mrs. R.:   Be more specific, Eric. Go into the paper. Show me where the content of L is more developed than the content of O. *(after Eric explains, continues questioning)* What else can we say about these two papers?

Jenny: I agree that L has more ideas in it, but O has a better beginning. It makes you want to read more.

Latisha: But L has a better vocabulary, and the sentences flow better. They follow each other very nicely.

Mrs. R.: What words did you particularly like, Latisha? And can you explain this flow of sentences that you like? What makes them follow each other nicely? (*after Latisha explains, continues the discussion comparing the two papers for a few more responses, making sure that students touch on some aspect of each category, always supporting their response with examples*)

Mrs. R.: Now what's the difference between these two papers and T and R? Most of you thought T was better. Why?

Sam: I think R is a 1 because the sentences run together, and you can't understand them. At least T has paragraphs.

Mrs. R.: What do you have on your Response Sheet under Content/ Organization for T? (*continues the discussion, asking students for responses in each category for papers T and R*)

Mrs. R.: We had a very good lesson today—an important one. Now, I'd like you to take a few minutes to think about what you personally got out of today's work. Jot down your thoughts in your journal or on a piece of notebook paper. (*gives them about three to four minutes*) Would anyone care to share?

Sara: It was fun scoring the paper.

Alexis: I liked the fact that we all agreed more or less on what was good and what wasn't.

Jenny: I liked arguing about the differences between papers. I still think O was better than L.

The important lesson here is not that everyone agree on what is a 4, 3, 2, or 1, but that students have begun to think and talk about content, organization, paragraphing, sentence structure, and the like. They are using the teacher's vocabulary and internalizing the elements of good writing.

The lessons in this chapter have begun the conversation about what constitutes good writing. In the next chapter, the conversation continues as students write and evaluate their own writing.

Chapter 2

Putting It Into Practice

Writing and Evaluating Our Own Work

Once your students have generated ideas about good writing and have had experience evaluating essays with their criteria, it's time for them to put what they've learned into practice. The following sequence of lessons is simply one way to use the sample essays in this book; feel free to adapt and experiment to suit your style and the needs of your students.

Lesson A: Writing in Response to a Prompt

Lesson B: Evaluating Sample Essays on the Same Prompt

Lesson C: Discussing the Evaluation Process—A Prime Teaching Opportunity

Lesson D: Writing an Effective Response Sheet

Lesson E: Reading and Scoring Class Work

It's time for your students to write. With the evaluation criteria they've generated in mind—and with a rubric and checklist in hand—they are ready to tackle their own writing assignment. Students will first write a response to one of the topics in this book. They will then evaluate the sample essays written on that topic to practice the process before they begin critiquing one another's essays. Next, students will score one another's papers, and finally, writers will have the chance to revise their original essays based on the class discussion and peer feedback.

Before class, assign a four-digit number to each student in your roll-book so that essays will be evaluated anonymously.

Lesson A: Writing in Response to a Prompt

In this lesson, as students respond to a prompt, encourage them to keep in mind all the ideas about good writing that the class has been discussing. Point out that their experience of writing and evaluating will help them perform better on in-class essays and state tests. The lesson might go something like this one:

Mrs. R.: You've been practicing how to score sample essays and have done very well. I think you're ready to take the next step, and that's to find out how your own writing measures up to what we feel makes a good essay. I've chosen a topic from this book for you to write about because the book also provides four examples of what other students have written on this same topic. That way, after I've collected your papers, we can read and score the examples from the book. Once we've discussed those papers, we'll see how well we can score our own papers. My question now is, "How do you think reading other students' papers can help you write better?"

Cora: Maybe we'll see their mistakes and we won't make the same ones.

Travis: I think it will make us more conscious of how we write.

Mrs. R.: Is that a good thing?

Travis: Sometimes. Then you know you have to write more or put things in another paragraph.

Jerri: You could also feel good about your writing. Maybe your ideas are better than theirs.

Mrs. R.: Very likely. Now, let's write. *(hands out composition paper)* When you get your paper, don't write your name on it. I'm going to give each of you a number that will identify your paper. You'll put that number in the upper right-hand corner. I want a number on your paper instead of your name because after we finish discussing the model papers, I'm going to distribute your papers at random so that nobody gets his or her own paper to read and nobody knows who has written what. And let's keep what we write to ourselves. That way the reader of your paper can respond honestly and fairly. You will have 30 minutes to write. I'll tell you when to start.

After students record their numbers, distribute copies of the question sheet and read aloud the directions at the top of the page. Then circulate around the room, making sure students are on task and answering individual questions without making writing decisions for them. At the end of 30 minutes, collect the papers. I have students write for 30 minutes because this is the usual time allotted for state assessments. Students should spend five minutes prewriting and five minutes proofreading.

Lesson B: Evaluating Sample Essays on the Same Prompt

In advance of this class session, make copies of the four sample essays based on the same topic your students have just written about. The papers should be stapled together at random so that students don't get the idea that the first paper is the best. I recommend allowing two, three, or even four days for the teacher-guided discussion and student responses.

On the first day of this lesson, students work in groups of four or five. The group discusses the packet of essays and assigns each essay a ranking from 4 to 1, using the Writing Checklist (on page 19) and either the simplified rubric from the Holistic Scoring Guide (page 18) or the Master Rubric (page 9). In the next lesson, after all of the groups have assigned a score to each essay, the whole class will come together to discuss the essays. After the class has discussed the rankings and responses to the samples, you should lead a discussion of any particular writing points you want to bring to your students' attention.

The implementation of group work followed by a whole-class discussion creates a dynamic learning environment. In particular, group reading and scoring allows more students to participate and encourages discussion.

Here's an example of how I've approached this next lesson:

Mrs. R.: Now that you've all written on the topic, let's read what other students have written. First, I'm going to divide the class into groups. *(arranges students at random in heterogeneous groups; once groups are organized in various locations of the classroom, asks one student in each group to be the reporter, the one who will tell the class what the group's responses are and will keep the group moving and not stuck on any one point; this organizing should take about 10 minutes)*

Mrs. R.: We're almost ready to read now. Does everyone have a Writing Checklist to help you evaluate the paper, a Holistic Scoring Guide in case you're not sure how to assign a score, and response sheets? *(distributes the set of model papers and repeats the directions.)* Now remember to read all the papers before you score any of them, just as we practiced a few days ago. Don't struggle too much over any one paper. In two or three minutes you can pretty much tell which score you'll give the paper. It will take a few more minutes to record your response. And, yes, you can change your mind. Your checklist will help you explain your responses. You have the rest of the period to read, record, and begin your group discussions. Tomorrow we'll see how each group rated the papers and their reasons for the ratings. *(as the groups go to work, moves from group to group answering questions individually and seeing that students are on track)*

Lesson C: Discussing the Evaluation Process—A Prime Teaching Opportunity

In this lesson, students' responses initiate the discussion; your role is to follow up and draw out points with the aid of the discussion prompts. The class begins with students regrouping as they were in the previous lesson. The discussion probably didn't get very far on the previous day. That's all right. This is a sample of what a general class response to the papers might sound like. It precedes the focus on each paper.

Mrs. R.:	I'm not sure how far you got yesterday. If I give each group about 15 minutes more for discussion, will that be enough time? *(waits for a response and makes an appropriate time decision, then circulates among the groups, explaining that it's not necessary for them to exhaust every possible answer)*
Mrs. R.:	Okay. How did it go? Let's hear from Latisha's group. How did your group score the papers?
Latisha:	We gave Paper K a 4, Paper I a 3, L a 2, and J got a 1.
Mrs. R.:	Did any other group come up with the same scores?
Sam:	No. We gave I a 4 and K a 3.
Jerri:	We came up with the same as Latisha's group.
Joe:	We didn't all agree. We argued about L and J.
Mrs. R.:	What do you mean?
Joe:	L has an opening and a conclusion and paragraphs, but one paragraph doesn't stick to the point, and she contradicts herself later on. We couldn't follow the meaning of some sentences. J isn't a good paper because the ideas are not developed and there are too many spelling mistakes, but the writer has some very good points to make.
Mrs. R.:	Well, we have our work cut out for us. Latisha, using your Response Sheet, tell us why you gave Paper K a 4.
Latisha:	We liked the opening paragraph. We thought it was a well-organized paper. The ending gave us some solutions. And there weren't any mistakes, I don't think. Also, paragraphs were developed.
Sam:	We thought the voice of the writer was very clear in Paper I. It was

as if he was talking to us. And he made good points, too. He wrote in paragraphs, and the ending was strong.

Jerri: We also liked I, but there were too many mistakes in it.

Mrs. R.:   Like?

Jerri: The writer forgot to put a question mark at the end of one sentence. There should also be commas, and there's a run-on sentence in the first paragraph.

Mrs. R.:   These are good responses. I see you're using your checklists to help you. Remember we don't all have to agree, but I'm pleased to see that we're all in the same ballpark. You and I know good writing when we read it.

Keep It Moving

There are two things to balance as students discuss the papers in their groups and as the teacher leads the class discussion: Don't rush the process and don't critique the papers to death. If a point isn't clearly made this time around, it will pop up again on the next paper. The same writing issues keep surfacing. Some students will get it the first time; others will get it at another time.

If there is at least 10 minutes left in the period, you can begin to use the discussion prompts that follow each essay, bearing in mind that they are only suggestions and this is not a list to be covered item by item. Feel free to change, add, ignore, or use your own questions, depending on the needs of your students. Here's what I might do:

Mrs. R.:   We've said Paper K is a well-organized paper. What exactly do we mean by that?

Sara: The opening paragraph tells you what the writer thinks and is going to say.

Mrs. R.:   Is there anything else on your checklist that has to do with organizing a paper?

Cora: Yes, paragraphs. They take up each idea.

Mrs. R.:   And is that it?

Eric: There should also be a good conclusion that comes from the ideas.

Mrs. R.:   Yes, and this paper has a good conclusion. Would you read it for us, Eric? (*after Eric reads, moves on to another point regarding content*)

We've also noticed some good things about the ideas in this essay, but some ideas could stand more development. I want you to pick one of the paragraphs you think could be better developed. Take a few minutes and rewrite that paragraph, keeping what the writer has already said but adding whatever details, information, or examples you think might make it better. *(gives students three or four minutes to write and then asks volunteers for responses)*

Quick Revision Practice

Whenever time allows, students should be asked to revise the essay being discussed. Revising one another's work will help them understand how they can revise their own work and teach them to work interdependently so that the learning process is seen as a class activity, not an individual activity.

Mrs. R.: Very good. Now, let's look at sentences. What did you write on your Response Sheet about this writer's sentence construction?

Cathy: I saw a fragment.

Mrs. R.: Where was that?

Cathy: In the last paragraph where the sentence begins with "Or."

Mrs. R.: How would you change that?

Cathy: I'd connect it to the sentence before it.

Mrs. R.: Good. Now, look at the last paragraph, the next-to-last sentence beginning with the word, "You." This sentence could be better if the two things the writer says about the organization, saving animals and the environment, were written in the same grammatical form. You could make the sentence stronger and get rid of unnecessary words. Would anyone like to try it? This is hard. It's called "parallel structure"—a good technique to learn because it pulls ideas together for the reader.

Allyson: I'm not sure. Do you mean something like "you are saving animals and helping the environment"?

Mrs. R.: Exactly. The "ing's" on the verbs link them. There's also another way to do it. "You are doing something to save these great animals and, at the same time, to help our environment." In this case, the word "to" in front of the verbs links them.

Mrs. R.: Let's move along to usage and mechanics. What did you write on your Response Sheet about the author's vocabulary?

Keep It Simple

Parallel structure is a difficult concept. It could be introduced in this lesson or reinforced if you've already taught it. Don't introduce more than one or two grammar, usage, or writing elements in a lesson. Use most of the time to reinforce earlier learning.

Brian: It was good.

Mrs. R.: Give me some examples of "good." What did you write down?

Brian: I just wrote "good."

Mrs. R.: Well, "good" isn't good enough. Look at the essay and pick out two or three examples of good vocabulary usage.

Brian: "Barbaric" and "abandoned."

Mrs. R.: That's what I want. On your response sheets, class, try to be specific. When you make a general statement, back it up with an example. *(since this is a relatively simple and satisfying exercise for students to do, asks for several more examples of good word choice)*

Mrs. R.: Are there any words or phrases you think could be better, more exact?

Sandy: Yes, I didn't like "and stuff."

Mrs. R.: Where was that?

Sandy: At the end of the first line in the second paragraph.

Mrs. R.: You're right. How could we change it?

Sandy: Maybe just put a period after "experiments."

Alexis: Or "people who abuse animals."

Mrs. R.: I like that. Let's look at the mechanics of the paper. What about the colon in the last paragraph? Is it correct?

Jeff: No, but I'm not sure why.

Carolyn: I don't think you need one.

Mrs. R.: Well, you have two ideas coming up that are solutions, so you can use a colon. But a colon before a list should follow a complete sentence. The list should not complete the verb "to be." Try writing a sentence that could go before that list.

Sally: "These are my suggestions" and then the colon?

Mrs. R.: That's one good possibility. Are there any others?

Joe: "My solutions would be the following ideas" and the colon after "ideas"? Would the rest be part of the same sentence?

Mrs. R.:   Yes. Both answers are good. And there may be other ideas as well. In writing, there are often many ways to solve a problem of sentence construction, grammar, usage, or mechanics.

By now you have surely gone into the next day's class. The three remaining papers should be reviewed following the patterns I have suggested.

Teaching Tips for Whole-Group Discussion

1. Select only a few items to focus on in each paper.
2. Have students resolve problems when possible: Let them rewrite a paragraph or a sentence, or come up with three ideas the writer did not think of.
3. Don't be afraid to teach. If there's a new concept, teach it.
4. Avoid making the teacher-guided lesson a lecture.
5. Move it along. Don't dwell on a single point or paper too long. You may spend two days discussing the remaining papers, but you don't want to go much longer.

Lesson D: Writing an Effective Response Sheet

The act of responding to writing teaches students more about writing than almost anything else. However, students need to be taught how to respond effectively. I recommend teaching this lesson the first time students write in response to a prompt from this book. It will give them examples of appropriate responses and show them the power of responses in helping writers to revise. As you monitor students' response sheets throughout the year, note the quality of their responses and reteach this lesson as necessary.

Begin with a discussion of what kind of feedback students would like to receive on their writing to make it stronger. Mention that while writers appreciate feedback, they are sensitive to critiques of their work. This simply means that responders need to think about the way they present their comments, keeping them constructive and specific while respecting the writer's point of view. Students need to remember that the goal of responding to writing is to help the writer write a stronger piece. I guide the discussion to cover the following points on writing effective responses:

Guidelines for Effective Responses
- Keep comments positive and specific. ("Last paragraph is okay, but opening needs to be more interesting.")

- Support comments with examples from text. ("Paragraph 2, first sentence. Word order is mixed up.")

- Offer alternatives. ("You could lead with a question.")

- Note where you would like more examples, details. ("Need more support in paragraph 3.")

- Note where the writing strays from the focus. ("Opening paragraph shouldn't go on about hunting. That's another paragraph.")

- Ask questions about what confuses you. ("Isn't poaching the same as illegal hunting?")

Once we've identified these ground rules, I share the sample essay on page 32 with students. I give everyone a copy of the paper and ask students to discuss it, using the criteria from the Writing Checklist. Then I distribute the Response Sheet on page 33 and discuss the comments. I might ask, "Are the responses here similar to the comments you just made?" I note how the comments are specific, stay focused on the writing, and offer suggestions for improvement.

Next I distribute copies of the revised essay, on page 34. We read this paper together and then discuss how the writer used the comments on the Response Sheet to revise. I ask questions like, "Can you find the changes in the revision that are based on the advice of the Response Sheet? How does this revision differ from the first draft?" I also invite them to evaluate the Response Sheet by asking questions like, "What did the reader mean by saying the writing wasn't 'direct?' Do you think the writer understood the comment? How do you know?" My point here is to help students see the connection between the comments readers make and the actions writer take.

This lesson makes a nice prelude to Lesson E, in which students read and evaluate their peers' work. It reminds students of the purpose and power of a well-done Response Sheet and keeps them focused on the writing task.

Give It Time

Be patient with the student who is trying to write a useful Response Sheet. This is a "teacher skill." It takes time and practice to learn. Occasionally, you can collect students' response sheets when they are working on the model papers in this book. You can then comment on their responses, give them a check or check plus or point out what else they need to notice and address. This way, students know that you're checking their progress and that the work counts. In addition to class participation, it's your way of assessing student learning.

Dear Animal Rights Group:

I am writing to tell you I would like to join your Animal Rights Group and help produce a Bill of Rights for animals. I believe that hunting rights, scientific experiments, etc. have endangered some species. Hunting, playing a major role. Illegal hunters and poachers should be stopped and brought up on charges.

Scientific experiments, I'm not too sure about. Some are for the good and only use lab rats. Though others, such as cosmetic testing, are somewhat cruel and inhumane.

I am in total belief of animals having a bill of rights and would like to support you in any way possible.

I believe there should be a law protecting animals from hunters, poachers, and unnecessary testing (such as cosmetics.)

Yet, new land developments cannot be stopped and are sometimes welcome. Unfortunatly it destroys animal's homes. I think there should be a law to allow a month or six weeks for the Humane Organizations or any other animals rights group to remove the animals and place them in good care.

As I have said before and will say again, I support you, and would like to help you in any way possible. Please inform me if I could be of any service to you.

I am pleased to know there are groups in the world who look out for those who cannot fend for themselves. You have my support. Keep up the good work!

Response Sheet

1. What is the code/name of the paper you are scoring? *4021 (Student identification number)*

2. Your score is ☐ **2** .

3. Using your Writing Checklist as a reference, explain how you scored this paper and why. Give one or two examples of the parts you think are good and those you think are weak or incorrect.

Content/Organization

Very repetitious

Too general—Ideas not fully developed. Needs more thinking, reasons and examples. Opening paragraph shouldn't go on about hunting. That's another paragraph. Last paragraph is OK but opening needs to be more interesting.

Sentence Construction

Fragment in par. 1

Paragraph 2, first sentence. Word order is mixed up. Also in Par. 2, couldn't you combine sentences?

Usage

The writing isn't direct. It's very wordy. The writer admits it himself, "As I said before and will say again."

Isn't "poaching" the same as illegal hunting?

In par. 5, "it" is wrong. What does it refer to?

Mechanics

Some unnecessary commas. Par. 1 after "hunting" par. 5 "Yet."

Capitalization mistakes, "Humane Organization." That's not their title.

Spelling—"unfortunately."

Dear Animal Rights Group:

I believe that hunting laws, scientific experiments and land developments are endangering the lives of many animal species. For these reasons I am interested in joining your group and helping to draft an Animal Bill of Rights.

Hunting laws play a major role. Illegal hunters should be brought to justice and put in jail if they continue to poach. Hunting animals for their fur should be stopped. There are plenty of substitutes on the market for fur. Some people will always want to hunt. After all, that's how people used to get food. But there doesn't have to be a long hunting season.

I'm not too sure about scientific experiments. Some are good and only use lab rats to find cures for human diseases. Others, such as cosmetic testing for mascara and eye makeup, use rabbits and ginny pigs and should abolished.

Yet new land developments cannot be stopped and are sometimes welcome. People like to go to malls. People also need houses. I think there could be a law to allow a month or six weeks for the SPCA or other animal protection groups to relocate the animals.

I'm pleased to know there are groups in the world like yours who look out for those who cannot fend for themselves. You have my support. Keep up the good work!

Lesson E: Reading and Scoring Class Work

This next lesson is devoted to the students' own compositions written before the holistic scoring session. This is better done individually rather than in groups. Distribute students' papers for reading and scoring, making sure the writer doesn't receive his or her own paper. You can tell students that this is what they have been practicing for. Students should have the sample packet of models on their desks so that they can refer to the models if they want to see how the paper they're reading matches up with a 4, a 3, a 2, or a 1. Students also need their checklists and response sheets handy, along with the Holistic Scoring Guide or Master Rubric. Talk to students about reading quietly and privately, about not making any marks on the papers they're reading, and, of course, about supporting what they write. Make sure that students understand that their comments need to be specific; an evaluation of the writing as "good" or "bad" will not help the writer improve his or her writing. Also, help students understand that constructive criticism identifies a problem and offers suggestions on how to improve; it does not merely criticize. Emphasize for the class that the long-term goal is for everyone to feel confident when responding to a prompt, either in class or on a test.

After the papers have been read and scored, they're ready to be returned to the writers. If you'd like each writer to receive two responses, redistribute the papers and repeat the procedure.

You may decide to return the papers to the writers on another day, especially if this is the first time you've tried this activity and you'd like to review the response sheets. I suggest letting writers read their original compositions before reading the response sheets. Give them a few minutes to reread what they have written and ask them to comment on their own work, using a Response Sheet or the questions that follow.

A Quick List of Questions for Writers

1. Was your content effective?
2. Were your ideas well developed?
3. How does your essay measure up to our checklist?
4. What problems did you run into?

After students have had an opportunity to revisit their papers and jot down some of their own observations, give them their reader's Response Sheet and allow time for them to read, absorb, and then discuss the writing issues that have emerged.

Mrs. R.: Compare the comments your reader made with what you yourself noticed. Were there many differences? Did you agree or disagree? You don't always have to agree with what someone says about your writing, but you have to pay attention to what is said and be able to support your point of view. Were the reader's remarks helpful? In what way? (*fosters a discussion by allowing others to share similar reactions or to comment on another student's reaction and thoughts*)

Mrs. R.: Now that all of you have been both writers and readers, I want you to take a few minutes to think about both of these experiences. Write down what you have learned about your own writing. Then write down the most valuable thing you learned about writing as a reader. (*gives class about five minutes to do this*) Let's hear some of your responses—either as writer or reader.

(*after the discussion*) I think you're all in great shape to revise this paper. Your first draft was just that—a draft of ideas, a very important step. Writing down our ideas helps us see what we want to say, and getting good feedback helps us make what we want to say clear to the reader.

I want you to take your first draft home with you along with the Response Sheet and revise your essay. Use what you've learned to make it clearer and more complete—in general, better. When you hand in your revision, please hand in your first draft and the Response Sheet as well.

Post-Writing Action

After listening to students' reflections on their own writing needs and after reading their revised compositions, you can now identify specific lessons to teach. Opportunities abound here for follow-up lessons on the use of linking words and phrases, parallel structure, pronoun agreement, paragraph development, sentence development, punctuation, and so on. Choose one or two specific lessons in composition to be given within the next few days. The cumulative effect of these lessons should be that students acquire the tools they need to write effectively and correctly in any situation.

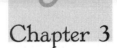

Chapter 3

Taking It Further

Where do we go from here? Helping students learn to write effectively is an ongoing, developmental process. As students mature, they learn to reason, to synthesize ideas, and, through guided practice, to recognize and articulate their understanding in writing.

But learning how to understand a prompt is an acquired skill that can be taught. Many students fail the state test or do poorly on it because they do not fully understand what the answer requires. This chapter provides a mini-lesson on how to understand a writing prompt, as well as offering additional topics for continued practice in writing.

Mini-Lesson: Understanding a Prompt

To help build students' skill in reading and understanding a prompt, you should spend a class period analyzing two prompts by discussing the kinds of questions students need to ask themselves as they plan a writing response.

First, distribute a copy of Sample Prompt #1 (page 38). Then, begin a discussion of the prompt, using the questions below. Write the questions on the board or on a handout:

1. What form of writing is the prompt asking for?

2. What ideas or arguments will the reader expect you to suggest? Would these points be good paragraph topics?

3. What does the prompt expect you to do?

4. Who is the audience for this essay? How does the audience affect your writing choices?

5. Write a quick, one-sentence answer to each question asked in the prompt. Use these answers to develop your outline and thesis.

After the class discussion, students need to try analyzing another prompt on their own. Distribute a copy of Sample Prompt #2 (page 38) and allow 10 minutes for students to answer the questions before you discuss their response as a class.

Sample Prompt #1

A substitute teacher for Ms. Jones, your math teacher, gave your class an important test, which the class knew to expect that day. Many students cheated openly on the test, and the substitute reported this to Ms. Jones, who held the whole class accountable and decided to lower everyone's mark on the test by one grade.

Since you were not among those who had cheated, you feel the punishment is unfair. Write Ms. Jones a letter explaining why you think her decision is unfair. Remember that your teacher feels everyone was at fault, even those who did not try to stop the cheating. How would you convince Ms. Jones that your solution is both fair and just?

Sample Prompt #2

Many years ago, a television executive described TV as a "wasteland," a lost opportunity to change our lives for the better.

Do you believe this is true? Do you think TV has affected our lives for better or worse? What do you watch? What do other people you know watch? Do you think your TV viewing affects your attitudes and behavior? If so, in what ways?

Write an article for a magazine like *TV Guide* or a local newspaper that features entertainment news. How would you reply to this critique of television? Explain your view with reasons and examples of specific programs.

Follow-Up Topics for Writing and Holistic Scoring

Here is a list of topics suitable for class writing assignments from grades 5 through 8, so student writers can continue to practice holistic scoring, using their checklists and responding to one another's papers. These prompts are based on the types of essays state tests typically address. For example, the personal narrative and persuasive essays are common essay types. Topics often deal with contemporary social issues as well. When helping students prepare for these tests, you might add some activities on newspaper reading and news program viewing. The more aware students are of general social issues, the more confident they will be in the testing situation.

Topics for Grades 5 Through 8

1. Think of a favorite place that you know well, one that you enjoy visiting, either alone or with friends. This should be a real place that you have been to. It could be in the city, somewhere in your neighborhood, in the countryside, or at the seashore.

   Write an article for a travel section in a magazine whose readers would be your age. Describe all the important details about the place. Tell how you first found it. Write about the different kinds of things you've done there. Be sure to tell why you think this place is so special.

2. Despite a national effort to educate young people, teenage drug addiction remains an alarming problem in our society. Can you explain why young people continue to use drugs and alcohol? Do you think your school is making a reasonable effort to deal with the problem? How could the community help solve the problem?

   Write an editorial on this subject for your school newspaper explaining why you think the problem still exists. Describe what you see as the school's current efforts to deal with the problem and recommend other actions the school might take. Suggest how the school could involve the community in helping young people reject drugs.

3. Pretend that you have been asked to write a book about something you know very well. It could be a hobby, a special interest, a sport. What subject would you choose and why?

   Write a letter to a publisher describing the subject, the audience that would most likely read about it, and why the publisher should publish it.

4. Environmental problems have become one of the major issues facing the world today. Some say, "Our bad habits have come back to haunt us." Acid rain, global warming, pollution, and the destruction of animal life have all resulted from our lack of understanding that how we live affects the earth we live on. Select one problem that particularly interests you and that you think can be solved.

   Write a letter to your state senator or representative explaining why you chose this problem and suggest at least three ways in which people, either individually or as a nation, could act to solve the problem.

5. A nine-year-old boy has been tried for murdering a seven-year-old girl. The National Center for Juvenile Justice reports that in the last 10 years, two-thirds of the states have toughened their laws for juveniles in response to the growing number of violent crimes committed by children under 15. Although people are shocked by the crimes kids commit, people are also divided about whether children should be treated as adult criminals and brought to trial.

   If you were a member of a debate panel, which argument would you personally support? Develop that argument with as many reasons as you can think of. Imagine what your opposition might say and argue against it.

6. Your town is being considered as a host community for a foreign student from a Middle Eastern country. The student could be a girl or a boy your age who comes from an average family. He or she would live with one or maybe a few different families for the next school year. You are the student representative on a committee of adults and civic leaders that will present a formal request explaining why your town would be the most desirable place for the student.

   As a member of the committee, what reasons would you give for hosting the foreign student? Consider the advantages your community might offer in terms of education, recreation, places of interest, and opportunities to exchange ideas. Be sure to consider what problems might arise and how the community could solve them.

Using Prompts
With Sample Essays

The following section contains six packets that can be reproduced for the class. Each packet contains an essay prompt and four sample essays in response to the prompt. Each sample essay is followed by a "Teacher's Guide" that features teacher Notes and Discussion Prompts. These guides serve as a teaching aid, and you may feel the need to supplement or curtail the ideas presented in the guides. I recommend that you read the entire packet before choosing that particular packet for your class. Also, you may want to read all of the packets before choosing any of them. Ideally, you would have time to read this entire section, decide which packets you want to use and how you will use them, and make all the copies necessary for their use prior to the beginning of the year, but when do teachers ever have enough time? With that in mind, I've made these as straightforward as possible.

The prompts are arranged from easiest to most difficult, with a range of grades 5 through 8. Depending on your students' abilities, you might want to start with a prompt from an earlier grade and end with one from a higher grade. Using these prompts and essays will help develop students' writing skills as well as build confidence in their ability to write in a timed-test situation. As their teacher, you will need to decide which set will best help your students begin building their confidence and their ability. You can follow the lesson sequence described on page 41. There's no one "right" way to use the essays and discussion prompts; they are simply a resource for you to use in your teaching.

This section of the text is based on a four-point scale, and the Appendix is based on a six-point scale. The essay prompts are the same for both sections.

A Guide to the Model Essays

Prompt Topic	Essay Letter	Score on Four-Point Scale	Page Number for Essay	Page Number for Discussion Prompts
Someone Important				
page 42	T	4	45	46
	X	3	47	48
	V	2	49	50
	S	1	52	53
Writing a Story				
page 42	D	4	54	55
	Y	3	56	57
	G	2	58	59
	Z	1	60	61
School Video				
page 43	W	4	62	63
	L	3	64	65
	N	2	66	67
	H	1	68	69
Problem at Your School				
page 43	M	4	71	72
	R	3	73	74
	E	2	76	77
	B	1	78	79
Animal Rights				
page 44	K	4	81	82
	I	3	83	84
	C	2	85	86
	J	1	87	88
Moral Dilemma				
page 44	O	4	89	90
	Q	3	92	93
	F	2	94	95
	A	1	96	97

Prompt #1: Someone Important

This is a class writing assignment designed to focus on building your awareness of the importance of content, organization, sentence construction, correct usage, and the mechanics of spelling and punctuation. Allow yourself a few minutes before you write to collect your thoughts. You may even write a brief outline. Leave a few minutes at the end of the writing time to proofread your paper and make any necessary corrections.

Think about someone who plays a special part in your life. This person could be a member of your family, a friend, or a neighbor—someone who might have done something important for you, or someone you just like to be with. If you were writing your autobiography, this person would have his or her own chapter.

Imagine writing your life story and write a chapter about this person. Tell what the relationship is between you and why it is special. Tell about one or two different experiences you have had together to show why the relationship is so important to you. Be sure to describe this person.

Prompt #2: Writing a Story

This is a class writing assignment designed to focus on building your awareness of the importance of content, organization, sentence construction, correct usage, and the mechanics of spelling and punctuation. Allow yourself a few minutes before you write to collect your thoughts. You may even write a brief outline. Leave a few minutes at the end of the writing time to proofread your paper and make any necessary corrections.

Your class is collecting stories for a book to be published by the end of the year. The editors will pick two stories written from the same opening sentence. Using the following opening sentence, let your imagination lead you into a story: "Sally looked out the window and saw the person she dreaded most coming up the front steps."

To be considered, your story should have a beginning, a middle, and an ending. It should include description as well as dialogue. But most of all, it should be interesting and have some original ideas in it.

Prompt #3: School Video

This is a class writing assignment designed to focus on building your awareness of the importance of content, organization, sentence construction, correct usage, and the mechanics of spelling and punctuation. Allow yourself a few minutes before you write to collect your thoughts. You may even write a brief outline. Leave a few minutes at the end of the writing time to proofread your paper and make any necessary corrections.

Your class has decided to make a 15-minute video about your school. The purpose of the video is to show the parents of new students the best things about the school.

Write a presentation to your class in which you include a statement of what you hope to achieve with this movie. Select three things about the school that you would highlight in the video and explain why.

Prompt #4: Problem at Your School

This is a class writing assignment designed to focus on building your awareness of the importance of content, organization, sentence construction, correct usage, and the mechanics of spelling and punctuation. Allow yourself a few minutes before you write to collect your thoughts. You may even write a brief outline. Leave a few minutes at the end of the writing time to proofread your paper and make any necessary corrections.

You have been asked to serve on a school committee made up of parents, students, and teachers. The purpose of the committee is to identify and help solve the major problems in your school. The problems may involve classes, extracurricular activities, the school program, even the building itself. From your point of view as a student, select what you think is a serious problem facing your school today. Explain why you think it is important to solve this problem and tell how you would solve it.

Write a report to the school committee describing the problem and explaining why it must be solved if the school is to improve. Propose your solution to the problem, in an effort to convince the committee that your recommendations will improve the school.

Prompt #5: Animal Rights

This is a class writing assignment designed to focus on building your awareness of the importance of content, organization, sentence construction, correct usage, and the mechanics of spelling and punctuation. Allow yourself a few minutes before you write to collect your thoughts. You may even write a brief outline. Leave a few minutes at the end of the writing time to proofread your paper and make any necessary corrections.

An animal rights group has asked you to join them to draft a Bill of Rights for Animals. The group believes that hunting rights, new land development that destroys animals' homes, and scientific experiments are a few of the things that have caused unnecessary suffering to animals and have endangered the existence of many species. Do you think animals are entitled to a bill of rights? What do you think the consequences of such a bill might be? Would you join the group?

Write a letter to the animal rights group stating your position about a Bill of Rights for Animals. Begin your letter with "Dear Members:" and tell them whether or not you will join them. Explain what you agree with or disagree with. Since your response could seriously affect the action this group takes, you want your position to be fully supported by logical reasoning and good examples.

Prompt #6: Moral Dilemma

This is a class writing assignment designed to focus on building your awareness of the importance of content, organization, sentence construction, correct usage, and the mechanics of spelling and punctuation. Allow yourself a few minutes before you write to collect your thoughts. You may even write a brief outline. Leave a few minutes at the end of the writing time to proofread your paper and make any necessary corrections.

One of your closest friends has asked you to help him (or her) convince his parents that he was at your house when, in fact, he was at a party with other friends of whom his parents disapprove. Your friend is afraid his (or her) parents will punish him severely if they find out. Now you have a problem you must solve—how best to help your friend. Although you value the friendship, you are uncomfortable about what you have been asked to do, but you would like to be able to help your friend.

Write a letter telling your friend whether or not you have decided to help him (or her). In either case, support your decision with good reasons for your action and suggest a way to solve the problem that will improve your friend's relationship with his parents and not endanger your friendship with him.

Prompt #1: Someone Important

Think about someone who plays a special part in your life. This person could be a member of your family, a friend, or a neighbor—someone who might have done something important for you, or someone you just like to be with. If you were writing your autobiography, this person would have his or her own chapter.

Imagine writing your life story and write a chapter about this person. Tell what the relationship is between you and why it is special. Tell about one or two different experiences you have had together to show why the relationship is so important to you. Be sure to describe this person.

The really special person in my life is my friend Nicole. She's funny, adventurous, bright and very pretty. We've known each other since kindergartan even though she is a year ahead of me in school. Our relationship has its ups and downs, and sometimes she's mean or fustrated with me. Mostly, however, she's like the sister I never had.

We think alike and agree on a lot of things. We're making up a musical that we want to put on as a school show. Nicole has written the story. I am writing the songs and she sings them. We also like doing girl stuff like painting our nails, listening to music, and talking to each other on the phone.

We've had days when we were mad at each other and didn't talk to each other until after lunch. Then one of our other friends would ask, "Are you two playing the silent game?" Then Nicole and I would laugh and make up.

She is always there for me and I trust her with my secrets. When I was crying about the way someone in class talked about me and not wanting to tell anyone, I told her. She understood how I felt and made me happy again. She told me if people are mean, I should just ignore them because I shouldn't let mean people win over me.

The best times we have are sleepovers when we share lots of stuff about school and growing up. We love to watch scarey movies and put on makeup, and pretend we're twins.

I'm never board when she's around. The only problem is, she's not around as much since they moved last year. That's the worse thing. When parents move and make it hard for special friends to be together.

Paper T

Score $\boxed{4}$

Notes	Discussion Prompts
Content/Organization	
1. The paper is well organized. The writer gives us an opening paragraph, a middle section, and an interesting ending.	1. What do we mean when we say a paper is well organized? Does this paper fit that description? Comment on the opening paragraph and the ending.
2. The writer understands how to use paragraphs.	2. Does each paragraph make a separate point?
3. The writer gives us some details, examples, and reasons for her friendship but could develop her ideas further.	3. What facts does the writer give us to explain why Nicole is special? Is there anything you would like to know more about?
Sentence Construction	
1. The writer knows how to combine related ideas into compound and complex sentences (par. 1, sent. 2 and 3; par. 2, sent. 1; par. 3, sent. 1; par. 4, sent. 1 and 3; par. 5, sent. 1).	1. Does the writer know how to combine ideas into compound or complex sentences?
2. There's a shift in sentence structure in paragraph 4. The verb forms should be parallel.	2. Are there any sentences that don't sound right or are confusing? What do you think the problem is, and how would you correct it?
3. The last sentence is a fragment.	3. Edit for run-ons or fragments.
Usage	
1. Except for her overuse of *stuff*, the writer's word choice is clear and effective.	1. How would you describe the writer's vocabulary? Is there anything you would change?
2. There's a pronoun without an antecedent in the last paragraph.	2. What's wrong with the use of *they* in the last paragraph? What should the writer have said?
Mechanics	
1. There are a few misspellings.	1. Proofread for spelling.
2. Except for a few comma errors, the writer's punctuation is correct.	2. Check the writer's punctuation. Do you find any errors? Explain.

Prompt #1: Someone Important

Think about someone who plays a special part in your life. This person could be a member of your family, a friend, or a neighbor—someone who might have done something important for you, or someone you just like to be with. If you were writing your autobiography, this person would have his or her own chapter.

Imagine writing your life story and write a chapter about this person. Tell what the relationship is between you and why it is special. Tell about one or two different experiences you have had together to show why the relationship is so important to you. Be sure to describe this person.

My Uncle Joe is special in my life. He is my Dad's younger brother and he's only about 10 years older than me, which makes us almost brothers. People say we even look alike. He's special because he always makes me laugh and he takes me to diferent places. He doesn't treat me like a kid.

He tells great stories like when he was in California or when he met a famous Hollywood movie star.

He took me to a country fair once, let me go on all the rides, and playing many of the games. Did you ever try to throw a ring around a bottle? I did and I won a prize.

Him and his girl friend Joan often come over on Sundays for dinner. We always have a great time when they come.

He's also very considrate. If I'm not feeling well or sad, he tries to make me feel better. He'll crack a joke or even bring me a present. Once I asked him to come to a baseball game I was playing on a Saturday and he came. He supports whatever I do. Sometimes he'll talk to me about things that bother me and tell me not to worry about it.

I think you can see what I mean when I say that my Uncle is special to me.

Paper X

Notes	Discussion Prompts
Content/Organization	
1. The writer knows how to organize a paper with an opening paragraph followed by a middle section and an ending paragraph.	1. Is the opening paragraph successful? What does it accomplish?
2. The writer understands the intention of a paragraph even though he doesn't give us enough details to develop most of them.	2. What is the focus of each paragraph? Do they each have sufficient information? What questions would you ask the writer?
3. The conclusion is weak.	3. What is your response to the conclusion?
4. The writer uses linking words to connect paragraphs and to lead the reader from one idea to the next. Find an example in the text.	4. Does the writer lead the reader from one idea to the next?
Sentence Construction	
1. The writer uses a variety of sentences and combines related ideas.	1. Does the essay have interesting sentence constructions? What makes them interesting?
2. The first sentence of paragraph 3 lacks parallel structure.	2. Look at the first sentence in paragraph 3. What do you see as the problem and how would you correct it?
Usage	
1. The word *like* is a preposition or a verb. It shouldn't be used to introduce a clause (par. 2).	1. We use the word *like* so often that we forget how it should be used. Is it used correctly in paragraph 2? Explain.
2. There are two errors with pronouns in the wrong case (par. 1 and 4).	2. Two pronouns are in the wrong case. Can you find them? Which pronouns should be used and why?
3. There is an agreement error between the pronoun *it* and its antecedent in the last sentence of paragraph 5.	3. Find the place where the word *it* is used. What is its antecedent? Which pronoun should be used?
Mechanics	
1. There are two spelling errors.	1. Proofread for spelling.
2. Commas are not always used correctly.	2. Check each use of the comma. Which ones are needed? Are there places where commas have been omitted? How does the placement of commas affect your understanding of the paper?
3. There are two words (*Dad's* and *Uncle*) that do not require capital letters.	3. Are all the capital letters necessary?

Paper V

Prompt #1: Someone Important

Think about someone who plays a special part in your life. This person could be a member of your family, a friend, or a neighbor—someone who might have done something important for you, or someone you just like to be with. If you were writing your autobiography, this person would have his or her own chapter.

Imagine writing your life story and write a chapter about this person. Tell what the relationship is between you and why it is special. Tell about one or two different experiences you have had together to show why the relationship is so important to you. Be sure to describe this person.

There is one person who stands out in my life above anyone else, that is my mom. She is always there when I need her. She is patient with me when I am down. She is willing to do anything to help me be succesful in life. She defends me and makes me happy.

My mom is very brave, and I look like her. She has brown hair and large brown eyes. She's not too tall, and she's very nice to everyone she meets.

One experience that made her special to me is one Christmas when she got me a present I wanted for years. Another time that made her special is when I felt sad and worthless. She gives me encouragment and good advise.

I have a good time with my mom. She takes me shopping with her. She lets me do a lot of stuff with her at home like baking a choclate cake. Of course I also sometimes have to clean my room, which is not too much fun. My mom never gets angry. She doesn't ever put her anger on me, unless I've done something really bad.

She's an awesome person. Nobody else I know can do ten things at once and still not go crazy.

Paper V

Score 2

Notes	Discussion Prompts
Content/Organization	

1. The opening paragraph is weak because it doesn't point the reader toward the content of the paper. The writer makes statements that are not developed in the paper.

2. Paragraph 2 lacks unity.

3. The writer introduces many ideas but does not develop them.

4. The conclusion could have been more effective if the writer had given us some examples of how busy her mother is.

---

1. What should the opening paragraph do for the reader? Does this paper's opening paragraph do those things?

2. Does each paragraph have a focus? Would you change any of them? Where and how?

3. Are the ideas well developed? What further questions would you ask the writer?

4. Are you satisfied with the last paragraph? Explain.

Sentence Construction

1. There is a run-on sentence right at the beginning.

2. Some sentences are not coherent; ideas are not logically or clearly related to each other (par. 2).

3. Several related ideas can be joined together to make more interesting and varied sentences.

4. Paragraph 3 has two sentences in which clauses follow the verb *is*. State-of-being verbs are completed by a predicate nominative. The second clause in each case is incorrectly joined to the first one. This is hard to explain in grammatical terms to young writers. It's important, however, to alert them to the fact that the first word in a clause after the verb *to be* has to be in the same form and has to be equal to the word that it relates to in the clause that precedes the verb *to be*.

---

1. Proofread for run-ons or fragments.

2. What's the problem with the sentences in paragraph 2? How would you change them?

3. What do you think of the writer's sentence construction? Do you think any sentences could be more interesting or clearer? Which ones? How would you address the problem?

4. Look at the first two sentences in paragraph 3. The clause that follows the word *is* needs a better connecting word because *is* acts like an equal sign. What comes after it should equal what comes before it. ("One experience" is not the same as "one Christmas"; a "time" is not a "when.") What would be a better way to connect the clauses in each of these sentences? You might even have to rewrite the sentence.

Usage

1. The verb tense in the last sentence of paragraph 3 is confusing. The reader assumes it should be *gave*.

---

1. Should the verb in the last sentence of paragraph 3 be in the present tense? Explain your answer.

Notes	Discussion Prompts
Usage, continued	
2. The writer's vocabulary is generally good. We might take exception with *stuff* and *awesome*.	2. Do you think the writer has an effective and accurate vocabulary? Which words do you especially like? Are there any words you would add or change?
Mechanics	
1. There are only a few misspellings. 2. There are a few misplaced commas.	1. Proofread for spelling. 2. Check the use of commas. Are they all needed? Are any omitted?

Prompt #1: Someone Important

Think about someone who plays a special part in your life. This person could be a member of your family, a friend, or a neighbor—someone who might have done something important for you, or someone you just like to be with. If you were writing your autobiography, this person would have his or her own chapter.

Imagine writing your life story and write a chapter about this person. Tell what the relationship is between you and why it is special. Tell about one or two different experiences you have had together to show why the relationship is so important to you. Be sure to describe this person.

The person that means the world to me is my little sister Georgia she is 3 years old. When she was born it was the best moment in my life. The only problem was I couldn't pick her up. She wieghd 12 pounds when she was born. But I still loved her and I do to this day. I can't imagine life without her. She makes me feel important because every day after school when I walk in the door she runs to me and gives me a big hug.

I cannot think of anybody who makes me feel so good. I can play with her and have a great time. We have many games we play together. I don't know what I would do without her. I love her to pieces. We had many moments I still remember, like the time you tried to feed our new kitten milk. It was the cutest think intel you through the kitten and the milk into the sink. I love to write down the funny things she says because we need to treaser these times together because I will not be 11 forever and she will not be a little kid forever.

Paper S

Teacher's Guide, Prompt #1

Notes	Discussion Prompts
Content/Organization	
1. There is a beginning, a middle, and an ending but the writer must learn to separate ideas into paragraphs.	1. What's the immediate problem you see in the organization of this essay? How would you solve it?
2. The prompt asks the writer to write a chapter about a special person in his or her life. The writer hasn't thought deeply enough about the possibilities of the subject.	2. Are you satisfied with how the author has answered the question? What more could you ask the writer about his or her relationship to Georgia? What title might you give the essay? Why are titles important?
Sentence Construction	
1. There are two run-on sentences and a third, the last one in the essay, could use a semicolon.	1. Proofread for run-on sentences or fragments. How would you change them?
2. The writer shifts sentence structure from third person to addressing his or her sister directly in the second person.	2. Is there any place where the sentence structure confuses you? What do you think the problem is and how would you solve it?
Usage	
1. In the second sentence (par. 1), the pronoun *it* lacks a reference.	1. In the second sentence of the first paragraph, what does the pronoun *it* refer to? Can you make the sentence clearer?
2. The writer makes some good word choices.	2. What's the purpose of the essay? Do you think the writer's word choice is effective? What examples can you give?
Mechanics	
1. There are several spelling errors.	1. Proofread for spelling.
2. There are comma errors.	2. Proofread for punctuation.

General Question for the Whole Packet

Did the writers really explore the possibilities of the question?

Prompt #2: Writing a Story

Your class is collecting stories for a book to be published by the end of the year. The editors will pick two stories written from the same opening sentence. Using the following opening sentence, let your imagination lead you into a story: "Sally looked out the window and saw the person she dreaded most coming up the front steps."

   To be considered, your story should have a beginning, a middle, and an ending. It should include description as well as dialogue. But most of all, it should be interesting and have some original ideas in it.

Sally refused to open the door when the bell rang. It was Tom, her mother's friend, someone Sally hated.

   "Open the door, honey," her mother called from upstairs.

   Sally let him in, barely said a word to him and then went to her room. She through herself on the bed and stared at the cieling. Tom was an older man maybe in his fifties, had grey brown hair and was just getting a little fat. Sally knew her mom liked him and they were talking about getting married but Sally hated him even though he bought her presents. Maybe it was because he never really talked to her.

   Sally fell asleep and had a dream about Tom being her dad. He never spoke to her. He only paid attention to her mom. Whenever Sally tried to speak, he would send her to her room or spank her. Then he and her mom would have a long talk about Sally's behavior that day. She never saw her mom much anymore, because her mom was either working or out with Tom. Sally had to make her own dinner usually fast food and not very good. She had tons of homework without any help from her parents who were always busy doing something else it was a very boring life for her.

   Suddenly Sally woke up. It was 4:30 in the afternoon she raced downstairs.

   "Tom was just going to leave," her mother said, "but I invited him to stay for dinner. Isn't that a good idea!"

Sally almost fainted, but she tried to smile. "I don't think we have enough meatloaf for all of us," she said.

   "Oh, don't worry about that," Tom said. "I'm a good cook. I can whip up something special for all of us in no time."

   And that night for dinner, Sally and her mom had the best meal with strawberry shortcake for desert. After dinner, Tom excused Sally from washing the dishes. "You probably have lots of homework," he said.

   Sally began to think maybe I could learn to like him a little better after all.

Notes	Discussion Prompts
Content/Organization	
1. This is a good story. There's an interesting and logical change in Sally from the beginning to the ending.	1. What do you think of the story? Given this situation, do you think the writer created a believable ending?
2. The story is well organized. Paragraphs are unified and focus on developing one idea at a time.	2. Is the story well developed? Does each paragraph serve a purpose?
3. The writer gives us descriptive and narrative detail.	3. Which details help us understand the story?
Sentence Construction	
1. The writer knows how to use and punctuate dialogue.	1. What does dialogue add to a story? Does the writer use and punctuate dialogue correctly?
2. The writer uses a variety of sentence structures (par. 1, sent. 2; par. 2, sent. 3 and 4; par. 4, sent. 3).	2. Has the writer been able to combine related ideas into interesting sentences? Give examples.
3. There are two run-on sentences.	3. Proofread for run-ons and fragments.
Usage	
1. The author writes well and uses a clear and effective vocabulary.	1. Who is the audience for this piece? Do you think the writer's choice of words is appropriate? effective? Give examples of what you mean.
2. There is one homonym error (par. 3, sent. 2).	2. Can you find the homonym mistake? What word did the writer intend to use?
Mechanics	
1. There are a few errors with comma placement and one piece of dialogue that needs quotation marks.	1. Proofread for correct punctuation.
2. There are two spelling mistakes, not counting *grey*, which is a correct variation of *gray*. The latter spelling is preferable. This could provide an interesting discussion.	2. Proofread for spelling.

Paper Y

Prompt #2: Writing a Story

Your class is collecting stories for a book to be published by the end of the year. The editors will pick two stories written from the same opening sentence. Using the following opening sentence, let your imagination lead you into a story: "Sally looked out the window and saw the person she dreaded most coming up the front steps."

To be considered, your story should have a beginning, a middle, and an ending. It should include description as well as dialogue. But most of all, it should be interesting and have some original ideas in it.

Oh No Billy Bragg! There was 2 feet of snow and there he was clumping up my front steps. He was the most boring person in the whole school. He always bragged about everything. Whatever you did he did better. He only came over to play with my computer.

"Sally," my mom said, "there's someone at the door for you."

"Yes, I see," I replied. I answered the door and Billy raced right up to my room. He was soaking wet. "What happened to you?" I asked. "Some kids threw snowballs at me but I'm so fast I got away before they could throw snow down my back."

"Let's get started," he said. I think my Spaceorama game is better than yours. I can knock out more Martians and score higher on my game than you can. You could use better software."

I tried to ignor him. I said, "Wait till you see what new things I can do with my Earthling game." Then I touched a magic key the zabitron, which made the picture so real you could walk right into it. And we did!

Billy was amazed. We felt ourselves walking in space. "How do you like this?" I said. "Wow!" was all he could say. We floated without gravidy. The air felt cold around us but we weren't cold. There were lots of red clouds and a reddish light coming from far away. Then we saw some very strange creatures slowly coming toward us. "What do we do now?" asked Billy.

The creatures were getting closer. They looked like green eggs moving on spiders legs. "Let's get away from here," Billy yelled.

Sally said, "Let's hide behind one of these clouds then they won't see us and we'll be able to see them closer." So they hid behind a cloud, but the creatures could walk right through the clouds.

Billy was shakeing with fear. "What's the matter," said Sally." Don't you like a little space walk, Earthling." Then when she saw that Billy was really fritened, Sally reached into her pocket and pulled out the Remote she had carried along with her. She pushed the Reverse button and suddenly Billy and her were back in her room.

Billy gasped for breath. "I can't believe what just happened." He even thanked Sally for bringing them back safely. He finally said, "I guess Earthling is better than Spaceorama. Before he left, Billy even mopped up all the wet snow he had dripped all over my floor.

Paper Y

Teacher's Guide, Prompt #2

Notes	Discussion Prompts
Content/Organization	

Notes	Discussion Prompts
1. It's a good rough draft of a story. There is a point to it with a character who changes by the end.	1. We read many outer space and science fiction stories. What do you think of this one? Explain your reasons. Would you add or change anything?
2. For the most part, the writer knows how to organize dialogue and narrative into paragraphs, even though there are a few paragraphing errors.	2. Has the writer paragraphed the dialogue and story correctly? Tell where you had any questions.
3. The writer gives us some description but could probably extend the story with more action and details.	3. This is just a first draft of a story. Where would you like to know more?

Notes	Discussion Prompts
Sentence Construction	

Notes	Discussion Prompts
1. Sentences are lively and varied.	1. Does the writer use a variety of sentences? Give examples.
2. There is one run-on sentence.	2. Sometimes in dialogue, writers can use fragments or run-ons. Proofread to see if any incomplete or run-on sentence is really necessary.
3. The writer switches the narrator's voice from first-person *I* to third-person *Sally* and *she*.	3. From whose point of view is the story being told? Is it told consistently from that point of view? Is it important to keep the point of view consistent? Why?

Notes	Discussion Prompts
Usage	

Notes	Discussion Prompts
1. There's a grammar error involving correct pronoun case (par. 9, sent. 5).	1. Does the story have any grammar errors?
2. The writer's word choice is clear and effective.	2. Is the word choice clear, believable, and effective?

Notes	Discussion Prompts
Mechanics	

Notes	Discussion Prompts
1. Several words are misspelled.	1. Proofread for spelling.
2. *No*, *remote* and *reverse* don't require capital letters.	2. Is capitalization correct? Explain.
3. Commas, an apostrophe, and a question mark are needed.	3. Proofread for accurate punctuation marks.

Prompt #2: Writing a Story

Your class is collecting stories for a book to be published by the end of the year. The editors will pick two stories written from the same opening sentence. Using the following opening sentence, let your imagination lead you into a story: "Sally looked out the window and saw the person she dreaded most coming up the front steps."

To be considered, your story should have a beginning, a middle, and an ending. It should include description as well as dialogue. But most of all, it should be interesting and have some original ideas in it.

Sally looked out the window and saw the person she dreaded most coming up the front steps. It was Mrs. Tuneout her piano teacher, she was so stricked but sometimes she can be cool.

Sally knew Mrs. Tuneout wanted her to play in the end of the year class recital but she didn't want the presire of it. Secretly she liked the idea of doing a solo and she knew she was realy good but she was also afraid of being on stage.

Today she was realy nervouse, because Mrs. Tuneout is making her play a very hard piece by Bach. This is the kind of piece that will take hours of practise. Sally thought maybe somebody else in the class could do it better. But she played it anyhow. Sally saw Mrs. Tuneout was very impresed.

Sally's mother walks into the room and complimented her. "Your playing so buetifully," she said, "I could listen all day."

"Oh, Mother," Sally thought,"Don't give me that stuff." But then in her heart she knew she had done a good job.

Mrs. Tuneout and Sally's mother went off into the next room were she knew her teacher was going to talk her mother into making her play at the recital."I won't do it," Sally said to herself. "No way!" "Suppose I make a mistake they will all laugh at me. Besides its too much work." Sally's mother and Mrs. Tuneout returned to the room smiling. "Mrs. Tuneout says you will do beutifully but its up to you. What do you want to do? " Sally looked at both of them. "O.K.," she gulped.

Paper G

Notes	Discussion Prompts
Content/Organization	
1. The writer tells a story with a beginning, a middle, and a surprising but believable ending.	1. Does each paragraph move the action along? Did you like the ending? Why?
2. The opening paragraph is weak because it simply repeats the question and then gives us some facts about the teacher that are not developed in the story.	2. Is the opening paragraph interesting? What should it do for the reader? Given the facts of this story, could you write a better one?
3. The last paragraph covers too much. It should be divided into three shorter ones.	3. Edit the story for correct paragraphing.
Sentence Construction	
1. There are run-on sentences.	1. Check for complete sentences.
2. The writer shifts verb tense unnecessarily, dislocating the reader's sense of time and place.	2. It's confusing to the reader when the writer shifts tenses unnecessarily. Can you find these verb tense shifts and correct them?
Usage	
1. Pronoun references in the first sentence of the last paragraph are confusing. The reader isn't sure to whom *she* and *her* refer.	1. Look at the last paragraph. How would you rewrite the first sentence to make sure that the reader knows to whom the pronouns refer?
2. There are two homonym errors: *its* (last par.) and *your* (par. 4).	2. Knowing what homonyms are, substitute the correct words for the mistaken ones the writer has used.
Mechanics	
1. Several words are misspelled.	1. Proofread for spelling.
2. Some commas are needed; others are used incorrectly.	2. Edit for comma use.

Prompt #2: Writing a Story

Your class is collecting stories for a book to be published by the end of the year. The editors will pick two stories written from the same opening sentence. Using the following opening sentence, let your imagination lead you into a story: "Sally looked out the window and saw the person she dreaded most coming up the front steps."

To be considered, your story should have a beginning, a middle, and an ending. It should include description as well as dialogue. But most of all, it should be interesting and have some original ideas in it.

It was Chelsea Brown the girl from across the street. What a bummer, I thought. I hope this is a dream. The doorbell rang. "Hunny will you get that? said my mother. "Yes," I said and opened the door. There she was wearing her desinger jeans and fur jacet and crying. "What's the matter,"I asked. "We have to move," she sniffled. I asked,"Where are you going?" "Australia." Party, I said under my breath. "What did you say," she sobbed. "Too bad," I said and kept my fingers crossed. "We will all miss you." My mom entered the room and saw Chelsea crying she asked what was the matter?Chelsea replied, "I have to move." "Why," she asked. "My dad got a big promotion and we have to move to Australia." "When will you have to go, " my mom asked. "Tomorrow," Chelsea cried even more. I almost jumped for joy, but my mom's face told me to behave. "We will all miss you, my mom said, and we hope you'll write to us, don't we, Sally?" "Oh yes, please write and tell us all about your new school. "I guess I'd better go home now,"Chelsea said. "My mom needs me to help with the packing." "Sally why don't you walk Chelsea home. Then you can say goodbye." "Good idea," I said. When we got to Chelsea's house, I said my goodbyes and tried not to skip all the way home.

Paper Z

Score 1

Notes	Discussion Prompts
Content/Organization	
1. The writer doesn't have control over paragraphing and punctuating dialogue. 2. The reader needs more information about the relationship between Chelsea and Sally to understand why Sally dislikes her.	1. Just looking at the story, what do you see as the immediate problem with organization? How would you reorganize it? 2. Does the story have enough information in it? What added details would make it better?
Sentence Construction	
1. There are run-on sentences. 2. There are a series of choppy simple sentences in the beginning. Some of the ideas could be expressed in more interesting compound or complex sentences.	1. Check for complete sentences. 2. Examine the structure of the opening sentences. Could they be improved?
Usage	
1. Pronoun reference is sometimes confusing. The writer uses *she* when the pronoun doesn't really refer to the last person speaking. 2. The author has a good vocabulary to describe Sally's feelings as well as Chelsea's.	1. Are pronoun references always clear? 2. Considering the purpose and the audience for this story, what is your response to the writer's choice of words? Explain.
Mechanics	
1. There are spelling errors. 2. Commas are needed in some situations other than those used in quotations. Also, questions within quotes need question marks and not commas.	1. Proofread for spelling. 2. Check for correct punctuation both within and outside of quotes.

General Question for the Whole Packet

Which specific details in any of these papers stayed with you?

Prompt #3: School Video

Your class has decided to make a 15-minute video about your school. The purpose of the video is to show the parents of new students the best things about the school.

Write a presentation to your class in which you include a statement of what you hope to achieve with this movie. Select three things about the school that you would highlight in the video and explain why.

Our movie about the Lincoln Middle School will show everyone how our school is tops in academics, athletics, and the arts. We hope that this movie will welcome new kids and make them a little less scared of their new school. It will also show the parents how happy their kids will be their while still being successful with their academics.

To begin with, the teachers here are exceptional. They use different methods and techniques to help kids understand their subjects and learn them. In Language Arts, kids are encouraged to read and practice vocabulary which is a crucial part of final exams. In Science, children do many fun experiments. In Mathematics, teachers have a way of making math fun and easy to remember. I would show teachers in their different classrooms.

Another great picture for the movie would be the new computer lab. All new I-mac computers, the cool colored ones! The computers are used by teachers for research as well as for computer classes.

The video would also show our sports program in action. In Physical Education, kids do everything from football to square dancing. There are lots of sports teams to be on, and kids can choose gymnastics, field hockey, football and powder-puff football for girls. We have tournaments in every sport and we could film one of them. After school you can always see either a soccer team or a lacrosse team pumped outside getting ready to win.

Some of the other classes a new student would really enjoy are in our Music Department. There are three different choices for students, and you can learn to sing in chorus, learn a new instrument in band or play a stringed instrument in orchestra. In the film we could show Dr. Washco, one of our fabulus teachers, conducting a rehersal. There are different bands and orchestras at Lincoln, one for each grade level. There's also a jazz band and a chamber music orchestra. The music programs are sensational. Each department holds their own concert for parents and friends, which is always wonderful.

Lincoln School is a wonderful place to learn and to have fun. My video would emphasize these things, but I would also invite parents to come in and see for themselves.

 Paper W   Score 4

Notes	Discussion Prompts
Content/Organization	

Notes	Discussion Prompts
1. The paper is well organized. The opening paragraph sets the tone and the ideas that succeeding paragraphs develop.	1. Do you think the ideas are well organized? Explain.
2. Paragraphs have topic sentences and are developed with relevant details.	2. When we say a paragraph is unified, what do we mean? Select one of the paragraphs and tell why it is or is not unified.
3. The writer uses transitional devices to link ideas.	3. Has the writer made it easy for the reader to follow ideas within a paragraph and from one paragraph to the next? How is that accomplished?

Sentence Construction

Notes	Discussion Prompts
1. The writer uses a variety of sentence structures but also has a sentence fragment.	1. Does the writer use a variety of sentence structures? Are they appropriate? Are there any fragments or run-ons?
2. The writer understands how to use parallel structure.	2. Parallel structure is a way of connecting ideas that belong together by using the same grammatical form. Can you find examples of this technique? How does it help the reader?
3. There's an unnecessary shift from third person to second person (par. 5, sent. 2).	3. Reread paragraph 5. Do you find a problem with the second sentence? Why is it a problem? How would you change it?

Usage

Notes	Discussion Prompts
1. There is a homonym error involving *their* and *there* (par. 1, last sent.).	1. Find the homonym error and replace it with the correct word.
2. Word choice is acceptable since the audience will be the writer's classmates.	2. Who is the audience? Is the writer's word choice appropriate and effective? Would you make any vocabulary changes?
3. There is an agreement error in the last sentence of paragraph 5.	3. Can you find any grammar errors in the paper?

Mechanics

Notes	Discussion Prompts
1. Spelling errors need correcting.	1. Proofread for spelling.
2. School subjects, excluding the names of languages, do not require capital letters.	2. Would you capitalize the names of subjects taught in school? Explain your answer.

Prompt #3: School Video

Your class has decided to make a 15-minute video about your school. The purpose of the video is to show the parents of new students the best things about the school.

Write a presentation to your class in which you include a statement of what you hope to achieve with this movie. Select three things about the school that you would highlight in the video and explain why.

Hello, this is Lincoln school speaking to you. This movie will highlight the best parts of this school and what it offers to young minds. I will try to put everything in it because there is nothing negative about it. Lincoln is a wonderful place to learn, to have fun, and to just be.

The teachers are incredible. All the teachers treat everyone with respect. Our teachers teach us geograph, mathematics, science, music, gym, Language arts, art, computers, and foriegn laguages. Each one of the teachers are kind, have extra help, and they have a good way of teaching.

There is no reason not to like any of the students here. They all have different and extravagant personalities. They are all smart, funny, and the oposite of dismal people.

The sports and recreation is also excellent and is fun to participate in. From games between students and teachers to everyday gym. Gym is also fun because it's a time to do sports and get away from schoolwork.

I like switching classes because it's hard being cramped up in the same classroom all day. Also it allows us to be in different envirments one classroom may be small and hot—and one may be big and cold. Being able to buy lunch allows you to try different things and have a hot lunch if you want to. It also lets you have more room in your backpack.

Our school holds many clubs and activities. Lincoln has a golf club, chess, drama, crafts, student government, debate spanish, french, and alot more. Lincoln holds a friday night activitity where we have dancing, basketball, and you can use a game room.

Lincoln school has achieved many things in the past we expect to achieve more in the future.

Paper L

Teacher's Guide, Prompt #3

Notes	Discussion Prompts
Content/Organization	
1. The opening starts off brightly with the writer addressing the audience in the video, but the idea gets lost in the rest of the paper.	1. Notice how the writer addresses the audience in the opening paragraph. How could he or she have continued to use this strategy throughout the paper?
2. Even knowing that the video's intention is to present the school in its most favorable light, some statements seem exaggerated.	2. Do you like the way the writer describes the teachers and the student body? Explain your answer.
3. The listing of subjects and activities is a dull way to present the school's offerings.	3. How would you describe the way the writer tells us about the school's offerings? What other ways might this information be presented?
Sentence Construction	
1. The writer has used parallel structure correctly in one place but needs it in another.	1. Where does the writer use parallel structure to link related ideas? Where else could the writer use parallel structure?
2. There are two run-on sentences and a fragment.	2. Proofread for complete sentences.
3. The writer often shifts the pronoun reference from first to second or third without a problem, except in one place, the last sentence in the next-to-last paragraph, where the subject shift is disruptive.	3. The writer often shifts the subject pronoun from *I* to *us* or *you*. Do any of these shifts disrupt the meaning? Would you change any of them either for clarity or emphasis?
Usage	
1. There's an agreement error between the singular subject *one* and the plural verb *are* (par. 2, last sent.), and another error between a plural subject and two singular verbs (par. 4, sent. 1).	1. Locate the grammar errors of agreement between subjects and predicates and correct them.
2. In one place, the pronoun *it* is used incorrectly to refer to different antecedents. In another place, the pronoun refers to a very general idea and should be replaced by a noun or a noun phrase.	2. Check the use of the pronoun *it*. Is it always being used correctly? Where do you find confusion, and how would you clarify the meaning?
3. Some word choices are questionable. What is meant when teachers "have extra help"? What is an "extravagant" personality? Does a school "hold" clubs?	3. Examine the writer's word choice. Do you find any words or phrases that are confusing or inexact? Would you make any changes?
Mechanics	
1. There are a few misspelled words.	1. Proofread for spelling.
2. There are several capitalization errors in which the writer has either not capitalized a proper noun or capitalized a word that doesn't need to be.	2. Proofread for correct capitalization.

Prompt #3: School Video

Your class has decided to make a 15-minute video about your school. The purpose of the video is to show the parents of new students the best things about the school.

Write a presentation to your class in which you include a statement of what you hope to achieve with this movie. Select three things about the school that you would highlight in the video and explain why.

Lincoln Middle School is a good school. It is a good place to learn. There are many activities and sports. Lincoln has wonderful teachers, and the academic standards at Lincoln are very high.

The teachers are nice and helpful. The students in Lincoln are also very nice. They are smart and achieve high standards. Each student sets there own goals and works throughout the year to achieve it. Students here learn a lot during the year.

The school has many activities like music and sports. In band students have a good time. Every year many kids join our sports program. Lincoln has a wide variety of sports to play. Football is one of the great sports to play here at Lincoln. There are lots of clubs including the Spanish Club. There are activities too. There was a fund raiser not to long ago.

Lincoln is the best school that I know of. Lincoln makes learning fun.

Teacher's Guide, Prompt #3

Notes	Discussion Prompts
Content/Organization	
1. Content is weak and underdeveloped. The writer dutifully gives one example for each statement but develops none of them.	1. Does the writer develop ideas adequately? Would you like more information? Pick three ideas and tell how you would develop them.
2. The second paragraph lacks unity.	2. Examine paragraphs for unity. What's the difference between paragraphs 2 and 3?
3. Although the writer explains why he or she likes the school, there's no attempt to address the question of making a video for parents.	3. Do you think the paper is a good response to the question? Explain your answer.
Sentence Construction	
1. The sentences are dull and lack variety. Except for one compound sentence, they are all simple sentences.	1. Does the writer use a variety of sentence constructions? How would you combine some of the related ideas?
2. Although the sentences lack variety, there are no run-ons or fragments.	2. Proofread for run-on sentences or fragments.
Usage	
1. There are two homonym errors (par. 2 and 3).	1. Are there any homonym errors?
2. The second paragraph has an agreement error.	2. Can you find and correct any mistakes in grammar?
Mechanics	
1. There are no errors in spelling or punctuation. The basic problem with this paper is lack of development.	1. Proofread for spelling and punctuation.

Prompt #3: School Video

Your class has decided to make a 15-minute video about your school. The purpose of the video is to show the parents of new students the best things about the school.

Write a presentation to your class in which you include a statement of what you hope to achieve with this movie. Select three things about the school that you would highlight in the video and explain why.

Lincoln has one of the best sports activities with two great teachers Mr. Cresco and Mr. Constantine they do sports like football, basketball, soccer and many other great activities. This is defenetly a place were I will do atheletics.

There is the academics, thay are hard but it is woarthwile. I was having trouble in Math it was hard for me but I went ever day after school to Ms. Morris now I have a "B."

There is the music department it sounds so good the wonderful music teacher is Ms. Larkin she does a really good job at leading the chorus.

There are clubs at Lincoln. You do all kinds of different stuff in there. We have parties and a lot of other things. Well this is Lincoln to me hope if you ever go hear you will like it as much as me.

Teacher's Guide, Prompt #3

Notes	Discussion Prompts
Content/Organization	

Notes	Discussion Prompts
1. Although the student writes in paragraphs, there is no opening paragraph to give us an overview of the writer's ideas. The last sentence could be a conclusion, but the writer has made it part of the last paragraph.	1. Is the paper well organized? Does it have a beginning, middle, and ending? Are ideas expressed in paragraphs?
2. The writer gives examples, but they are minimal or vague.	2. Is there enough information about each of the ideas? What would you like to know more about?
3. The writer ignores the idea that this is a statement about a projected video.	3. Has the writer answered the question? What more is needed?

Sentence Construction

Notes	Discussion Prompts
1. The writer does not have control over sentence structure.	1. Proofread for run-on sentences.
2. Sentences lack variety. Paragraphs 2, 3, and 4 all begin the same way.	2. Notice how each of the three main paragraphs begins. What topic sentence would you write for each of these paragraphs?
3. In the last paragraph, the writer changes the subject from *you* to *we*.	3. In the last paragraph, the writer begins with *you* as a subject and then switches to *we*. Would you correct that? Why?

Usage

Notes	Discussion Prompts
1. *It* is used as a weak pronoun reference (par. 3).	1. Examine the use of the pronoun *it*. Where is its use acceptable, and where does it create vagueness?
2. There are agreement problems in the first sentence of paragraph 2 and an error in pronoun case in the last sentence.	2. Do you find any grammar errors?
3. There is one homonym mistake (last sent.).	3. Find the homonym error and correct it.
4. The writer is not careful enough about word choice.	4. Do you think the word choice is interesting enough to make students pick this video? What words would you change or add?

Notes	Discussion Prompts
Mechanics	
1. There are spelling errors. 2. Even when the run-on sentences are corrected, there are still important places for commas.	1. Proofread for spelling. 2. After correcting run-on sentences, do you still find places that need commas? Explain.

General Question for the Whole Packet

Which paper(s) gave the best examples of how grammar affects meaning?

Prompt #4: Problem at Your School

You have been asked to serve on a school committee made up of parents, students, and teachers. The purpose of the committee is to identify and help solve the major problems in your school. The problems may involve classes, report cards, extracurricular activities, clubs, even the building itself. From your point of view as a student, select what you think is a serious problem facing your school today. Explain why you think it is important to solve this problem and tell how you would solve it.

Write a report to the school committee describing the problem and explaining why it must be solved if the school is to improve. Propose your solution to the problem, in an effort to convince the committee that your recommendations will improve the school.

One of the most serious problems facing not only our school but our nation is that of ignorance about the heritage and culture of other people. I believe that one of the main causes of racial tensions and prejudice stems from the lack of information about cultures different from the majority. This ignorance can be eliminated with a subtle but giant change: we must create broader studies about different cultures in our curriculum.

There are many good reasons for broadening the curriculum. We need the understanding that is created when we learn about anothers culture. If we don't, then we will grow to believe the stereotypes and look at them as facts. We need the respect that comes from understanding that there were other civilizations besides the one's on the European continent. We need to understand that the Africans, the Chinese, and the

Indians, did not just wait for a European explorer to come and civilize them; they already had civilizations that were highly advanced.

If our school is to prepare us for life in a multicultural world, then we must learn more about different cultures. The world history we learn isn't really world history; it's just about one part of the world. Unless we change our curriculum, most students will only get the chance to learn about Asia or India or Africa if they go to college and take special courses.

Another reason for broadening the curriculum is that in our school there are a vast range of ethnic, religious, and racial groups. To the educated person this range of groups is fantastic; but to the uneducated person, it creates tension. Some people think they're better than others because their skin is white and they come from a European background. Other people become angry because they feel left out of school and must learn only about the culture and accomplishments of the majority, never about their own. People resent being left out and looked down upon. These attitudes cause racial tension. We see this problem in many places in our country, not just in our school.

Although I can't say that this will solve all the problems between different racial and cultural groups, I believe it is one step that will help lead our students into a future of understanding from a dismal past of ignorance.

Paper M

Notes	Discussion Prompts
Content/Organization	
1. Content is focused on one idea that is supported by mature reasoning and examples.	1. What is the central idea of this paper? Which reasons and examples support it?
2. The paper is organized with an introduction, a middle section that develops the idea, and a conclusion based on the information the writer has given.	2. How does the way the paragraphs are organized contribute to the reader's understanding?
3. Paragraphs are unified.	3. What is meant by "paragraph unity"? Find a good example.
4. Ideas are developed in a logical sequence leading to the conclusion.	4. Are the ideas in a logical order? Do they lead to the writer's conclusion?
5. Transitional devices and careful repetition help to link and reinforce ideas.	5. Can you identify some of the transitional devices used in this paper? How do they help you understand the ideas?
Sentence Construction	
1. Using correct punctuation, the writer knows how to combine several related ideas to give a variety of sentence constructions.	1. How do these sentence constructions help you understand the writer's ideas?
2. An incomplete comparison (the last few words of sent. 2 in par. 1), a misplaced modifier (last sent. in par. 1), and some words missing in the predicate (sent. 3 in par. 2) interfere with meaning.	2. Are there any phrases or sentences that you had trouble with? Did they interfere with your complete understanding of the sentence? How would you change those phrases or sentences?
Usage	
1. With few exceptions, the student's choice of words is excellent and appropriate for the occasion and the audience.	1. Consider the purpose of this paper and the audience for whom it was intended. Do you think the vocabulary is effective and appropriate?
2. Grammar errors appear in subject-verb agreement (par. 4) and in weak pronoun references (*it* and *this*) in the last two paragraphs.	2. Are there any errors in grammar? How do grammar errors affect your understanding of the sentence? What would you change to be more correct or exact?
Mechanics	
1. There are some punctuation errors (apostrophe errors in par. 2, comma errors in par. 2 and par. 4).	1. Are there any errors in punctuation? Do they interfere with your understanding of ideas? How would you correct them?
2. The student makes only one spelling error (in par. 4).	2. Are there any misspelled words or errors in capitalization?

Paper R

Prompt #4: Problem at Your School

You have been asked to serve on a school committee made up of parents, students, and teachers. The purpose of the committee is to identify and help solve the major problems in your school. The problems may involve classes, report cards, extracurricular activities, clubs, even the building itself. From your point of view as a student, select what you think is a serious problem facing your school today. Explain why you think it is important to solve this problem and tell how you would solve it.

Write a report to the school committee describing the problem and explaining why it must be solved if the school is to improve. Propose your solution to the problem, in an effort to convince the committee that your recommendations will improve the school.

As I examined the many problems facing our school, I came to the conclusion that the treatment of athletes is rather unfair.

There are a few reasons which are noteworthy. First, the amount of time after school given to students, who participate in athletics, is paltry. On a typical day, an athlete might have practice at 3:45. This leaves an athlete approximately 25 minutes after school before they have to journey to their practice site. Not factored into this equation, is the fact that a teacher is usually helping one or two more students while the athlete is also requesting help.

To give you an example of how muddled an athlete's schedule can be, I followed around an athlete named "John" who participates on the basketball team.

John's schedule began rather normally. He went to all of his classes, taking notes, and behaving like a typical student. A problem arose in John's math class where he didn't understand the day's lesson. After school, he went for help, but much to his chagrin, there were two other students already receiving extra guidance. As John patiently waited, and time ticked away, he became increasingly anxious, that he would have to face the wrath of his coach if he were late to practice. Hence, he left before he could receive the help he dearly needed.

When John arrived at practice, the coach reprimanded him for his tardiness. Unable to explain his plight, John was forced to run extra laps and to miss the coach's strategy for the next upcoming game. This forced John to be scratched from his usual starting lineup position.

As John was picked up from practice, he was both depressed and tired, as he had no comprehension of his math and no starting lineup spot.

In conclusion, I think our school should make an increased effort to provide extra help for athletes; thus greatly improving their view of school and their pursuit of an education. I hope we can improve this plight.

Teacher's Guide, Prompt #4

Notes	Discussion Prompts
Content/Organization	

Notes	Discussion Prompts
1. The paper clearly has a beginning, a middle, and an ending; however, the opening paragraph is weak, the argument is based on only one example, and the conclusion is a summary with only one story to support it.	1. What are the strengths and weaknesses in the content of this paper? Explain your answer.
2. One of the main flaws in this paper is its tone. The language is inflated to impress the reader. The occasion and the audience require good, formal English, not to be confused with big words that are used to sound important but actually take away from the sincerity of the argument.	2. How would you describe the tone of this paper, and how does it affect you as a reader? Which words or phrases would you change?
3. The writer provides transitions that tell the story in a logical narrative sequence.	3. How does the writer link related ideas?
4. The writer describes the problem but offers no ideas as to what the school can reasonably do about the situation.	4. Does the writer fulfill the assignment? What suggestions would you offer?

Sentence Construction	
1. The writer has great skill constructing sentences and uses a variety of sentence forms: simple, complex, compound-complex. Paragraph 4 contains a good example.	1. How does sentence variety move ideas along and keep the reader interested?
2. Parallel structure creates effective and clear sentences (par. 5, sent. 2; par. 7, sent. 1).	2. Sometimes the writer is very good at condensing ideas and linking them. Can you find some examples?
3. An incorrect subordinating conjunction (par. 6) does not show the exact relationship between clauses.	3. As is a subordinating conjunction. Is it used correctly in paragraph 6? Is there a better conjunction to connect the clauses?

Usage	
1. An error in pronoun agreement confuses the reader (par. 2).	1. Are there any grammar errors? How do they interfere with your understanding? How would you correct them?
2. Indefinite pronoun references create vague writing (par. 2 and 5).	2. The word *this* is used twice as a pronoun. Does it have a clear reference? How could you clarify the meaning?

Notes	Discussion Prompts
Usage, continued	
3. Although this writer obviously has a good vocabulary, in the attempt to sound important, he or she sometimes uses words incorrectly (*participates*, *dearly*, *plight*).	3. Sometimes in trying to sound important, we actually use the wrong word. Are there any words that you think are really inaccurate?
Mechanics	
1. The writer uses commas unnecessarily.	1. Are all the commas necessary? Which ones would you keep and why?

Prompt #4: Problem at Your School

You have been asked to serve on a school committee made up of parents, students, and teachers. The purpose of the committee is to identify and help solve the major problems in your school. The problems may involve classes, report cards, extracurricular activities, clubs, even the building itself. From your point of view as a student, select what you think is a serious problem facing your school today. Explain why you think it is important to solve this problem and tell how you would solve it.

Write a report to the school committee describing the problem and explaining why it must be solved if the school is to improve. Propose your solution to the problem, in an effort to convince the committee that your recommendations will improve the school.

I feel we need students to participate in more extra-curricular activities. Too many students are not involved in our school and it is important for students to belong to clubs or play sports because that shows their school spirit and that they go to this school. It also helps them in school because if they want to play a sport they have to keep their grades up and that makes them work harder. Also you feel a sense of belonging and people appreciate you.

Even though we have alot of clubs we could have a few more and maybe we could advertize and announce when meetings of clubs are more times so more students could know when clubs and tryouts are.

Many students are all ready involved and show their school spirit and I think those students should go and persuade other students to join their club.

I feel it is always good when you participate in activities because it gives you a sense of who you are and shows that students are proud to represent their school. Students show their enthusiasm through clubs and teams. It shows that you care about your teamates and hope they do good.

Maybe if we asked students what kind of clubs they would like to join we would have a better idea of the kind of clubs to have. The first step is to find out what students are interested in and then to find volunters who want to run the club.

This could be the beginning of new school spirit and school unity.

Paper E

Score 2

Notes	Discussion Prompts
Content/Organization	
1. The opening paragraph is a weak statement; ideas are not strongly linked and presented to the reader as the focus of this paper.	1. What do you think are the main problems with the opening paragraph? Try to rewrite it to correct some of these failings.
2. Paragraphing is weak. Ideas that should go together are separated (in par. 2 and 5 and in par. 3 and 4).	2. List the points brought up in each paragraph. Do you find any ideas that belong together but are written in separate paragraphs?
3. The content is too general; the reader feels a lack of information about the extracurricular program and only the beginning of a few suggestions. There are no facts or examples that would make the reader see a lack of school spirit or unity.	3. What do you think is the main problem with the content? Where would you make additions or changes?
Sentence Construction	
1. Faulty coordination blurs the meaning. Ideas should either be subordinated into clauses and phrases or separated into sentences.	1. What's the purpose of using *and* to connect ideas? This writer uses *and* throughout the paper. Are there any places where a better conjunction could be used? Explain your answer.
2. A run-on sentence and faulty word order (par. 2) make statements difficult to understand.	2. Where do you see problems in paragraph 2? Do they interfere with meaning? How would you make the idea clearer?
3. There are unnecessary pronoun shifts.	3. Look at the personal pronouns in paragraphs 1 and 4. How does the shift from one pronoun to another affect your understanding? What would you like to change and why?
Usage	
1. Indefinite pronoun references confuse readers.	1. Why do you have to be careful when you use the word *it*? Are there places where the word should be replaced? Why?
2. Words must agree with each other in number (par. 5).	2. Can you find any grammar errors? How would you correct them?
3. The writer needs an adverb, not an adjective in paragraph 3.	3. Is *all ready* the correct choice of words in paragraph 3? Why?
Mechanics	
1. The writer needs to understand the use of commas.	1. As the paper now reads, where would you place commas? How would that help you to understand the ideas in the paper?
2. There are several spelling errors.	2. Are there any spelling errors? How would you correct them?

Prompt #4: Problem at Your School

You have been asked to serve on a school committee made up of parents, students, and teachers. The purpose of the committee is to identify and help solve the major problems in your school. The problems may involve classes, report cards, extracurricular activities, clubs, even the building itself. From your point of view as a student, select what you think is a serious problem facing your school today. Explain why you think it is important to solve this problem and tell how you would solve it.

Write a report to the school committee describing the problem and explaining why it must be solved if the school is to improve. Propose your solution to the problem, in an effort to convince the committee that your recommendations will improve the school.

I think that there should be days that classes do good deeds for there school, like repainting walls, repair and clean the lockers, to sweep the halls, and clean up around the school ground. This would need everybody to make it happen. Every student would have to respect the property of the school, and to help others if they step out of line.

Our school has grafete, and all kinds of stuff in the halls, and there is not enough custodens to rome around the halls looking for any dirt, or to see if the halls need a sweeping job. Students have picked up on the problem, and wrote about it in the school newspaper. See, a kid like me, thinking about this alone can't do nothing about it. If we could agree on a procedure me and others in the school would get in and do it.

Think about it. If your gonna be in a school for all this time wouldn't you want to keep it clean.?

Paper B

Notes	Discussion Prompts
Content/Organization	

Notes	Discussion Prompts
1. Although there are many errors in this paper, the student does focus on one topic, answers the question, and has a sense of organization with a beginning, a middle, and an ending.	1. Despite many writing errors, the author does know how to organize a paper. What positive things about content and organization can you see?
2. The writer has a bold idea but doesn't develop it. We need more facts about the problem and more thinking about the proposal.	2. How would you develop each of the ideas the writer suggests?
3. Paragraph 2 lacks unity. Each sentence seems to be a separate idea, suitable for a paragraph of its own.	3. Paragraph 2 has at least three ideas in it. Select one of them and tell how you would develop it.

Sentence Construction	
1. In paragraph 1, the first sentence needs parallel structure to unite and coordinate ideas.	1. How could you link the related ideas in paragraph 1 to make a more coherent and interesting sentence?
2. Ideas should be subordinated to or separated from each other instead of being joined by *and* (par. 2, sent. 1).	2. What's the problem with the way ideas are connected to each other in the first sentence of paragraph 2? What would you do to correct it? Why is it important to choose the right connecting words?

Usage	
1. Homonym errors confuse the reader.	1. How do homonym errors affect reading? Are there any homonym errors in this paper? What should the correct spelling be?
2. Indefinite pronouns create vagueness.	2. Do you really understand the meaning of the second sentence in paragraph 1? Which words cause the confusion? Which words would you substitute?
3. Colloquial words and sub-standard usage create shifts in tone.	3. Who is the audience for this paper? Is the language appropriate? Change whatever you think is necessary and explain why.
4. There are three grammar errors in paragraph 2.	4. What grammar errors have you found? What effect do they have on your understanding and on your response to the writing?

Notes	Discussion Prompts
Mechanics	
1. Spelling errors distract the reader.	1. Besides the homonym errors, what spelling errors distract you from understanding? How would you correct them?
2. Unnecessary commas and comma omissions make reading difficult.	2. Proofread for commas. How does the placement of commas or the omission of commas interfere with your understanding?

General Question for the Whole Packet

In your reading and discussion of these papers, what was the single most important thing that either made you want to read on or to stop?

Prompt #5: Animal Rights

An animal rights group has asked you to join them to draft a Bill of Rights for Animals. The group believes that hunting rights, new land development that destroys animals' homes, and scientific experiments are a few of the things that have caused unnecessary suffering to animals and have endangered the existence of many species. Do you think animals are entitled to a bill of rights? What do you think the consequences of such a bill might be? Would you join the group?

Write a letter to the animal rights group stating your position about a Bill of Rights for Animals. Begin your letter with "Dear Members:" and tell them whether or not you will join them. Explain what you agree with or disagree with. Since your response could seriously affect the action this group takes, you want your position to be fully supported by logical reasoning and good examples.

Dear Members:

I respect your Animal Rights Group greatly and fully support it. The idea for a Bill of Rights for Animals is an excellent one. I believe that animals are legally entitled to a bill of rights because they are living creatures and should be allowed to live in peace without being tortured, deprived of their natural homes, or murdered by other living creatures. Finally an organization like yours has come up with an idea to help these suffering animals.

The Bill of Rights should help save the animals from lab experiments and such. I think these experiments are cruel and barbaric. There may be a lot of good that comes from them, but they kill living things in the process. Scientists must come up with another way to test these products.

The Bill of rights should include laws that will set aside certain areas for all animals, protecting them from hunters as well as land developers. These areas should be suited toward each animal's purposes. There should also be more shelters for abandoned and wounded animals in my opinion.

I see many problems that will arise because of this. First of all, what will scientists use in place of the animals that they experiment on? Or where will people build new houses if they don't cut down the forests? How about money? It takes a lot financially to face these situations.

Some solutions might be: to simulate animal and human eyes for making working models. Or maybe to make condominiums which don't take up as much space as large houses. As I mentioned earlier, we must also help relocate animals to protect them. I will gladly join your group. You are doing something to save these great animals and, at the same time, you are also helping our environment. It is a group I will be proud to join.

Yours truly,
Chris Jackson

Paper K

Score **4**

Notes	Discussion Prompts
Content/Organization	
1. The writer clearly knows how to organize a composition. The opening paragraph establishes a point of view, a middle section develops it, and a final paragraph ends it.	1. How does the organization of this paper help you understand it?
2. Although the writer uses paragraphs effectively to organize ideas, some of the ideas need more development (par. 2, lab experiments; par. 3, already protected areas).	2. Are all paragraphs sufficiently developed? Could you add details to any of them?
3. The writer tries to answer each of the issues raised by the question.	3. What makes the content of this paper interesting to read?
4. Avoid overuse of the first-person pronoun in an expository paper because it creates wordiness and weakens the argument.	4. What's your response to the phrase *in my opinion* at the end of paragraph 3? Are there any other examples of the use of *I* that could be changed?
Sentence Construction	
1. Some ideas need to be combined into stronger statements that would connect them to each other and reduce wordiness (par. 2, sent. 1 and sent. 2; par. 3, sent. 1 and 2).	1. How would you combine some of the related ideas? What effect does combining ideas have on your understanding of the sentence?
2. Occasionally fragments that should be part of the preceding statement appear on their own.	2. Are there any fragments? How would you correct them?
3. Parallel structure would help to coordinate several ideas.	3. Sentence 3 in the first paragraph uses parallel structure? How does that help the reader? Is there anyplace where parallel structure could help the sentence?
Usage	
1. Although the writer's choice of words is generally good, some words are inexact and create vagueness (*idea*, repeated in par. 1).	1. What's the purpose of this letter? Do you think the writer's choice of words is effective? Would you change any of them?
2. Indefinite pronoun references like *this* and *they* create vagueness (par. 4).	2. Which words in paragraph 4 create a sense of vagueness? What alternatives do you have?
Mechanics	
1. The colon should be used after a complete statement that comes before a list (last par., sent. 1).	1. Is the use of the colon in the last paragraph correct? Explain.
2. A comma should follow the word *Finally* in the first paragraph.	2. Proofread the paper for punctuation.

Prompt #5: Animal Rights

An animal rights group has asked you to join them to draft a Bill of Rights for Animals. The group believes that hunting rights, new land development that destroys animals' homes, and scientific experiments are a few of the things that have caused unnecessary suffering to animals and have endangered the existence of many species. Do you think animals are entitled to a bill of rights? What do you think the consequences of such a bill might be? Would you join the group?

Write a letter to the animal rights group stating your position about a Bill of Rights for Animals. Begin your letter with "Dear Members:" and tell them whether or not you will join them. Explain what you agree with or disagree with. Since your response could seriously affect the action this group takes, you want your position to be fully supported by logical reasoning and good examples.

Dear Members:

I do not think I'm the right one to ask for this task. I think some of the points you express are cruel to animals but some are necessary to the paying customer. Let's say you just graduated college and needed a home. Where would you be able to live if no new homes were built. And if by chance you found one, the cost would be extremly high. Our nation is growing we need new land developements.

Scientific experiments are also neccessary to our survival unless of course you and your comittee would like to donate your bodies to science. Would you try a medicine that might have deadly side effects. Cures for thought incurable diseases were found by experimenting on Laboratory animals. How would you like it if a member of your family died from a disease because there was no cure, but no animals were dead.

Hunting can be a good thing. Some people have to hunt for food. If your Mother and Father were poor and the only means to support themselves was an old rifle, you wouldn't see it as that bad. Besides, if there is no hunting certain animals' population might become too large, and then there would be another problem to face.

I hope I've made myself quite clear without angering you too much but I feel quite strongly on this matter. I'm not saying your right or I'm right I'm just saying I think humans are a little more important than animals and people should look at all sides before making a decision. You might be suprised when you argue your point and realize you might not have seen all the sides to the matter.

Yours truly,
Ben Watson

Paper I

Notes	Discussion Prompts

Content/Organization

Notes	Discussion Prompts
1. The writer has a clear and consistent point of view that answers each part of the question.	1. Does the writer have solid arguments to support his point of view?
2. The writer knows how to organize a paper with a beginning, a middle section, and an ending, and he uses topic sentences well.	2. Do you find the ending satisfactory? Explain your answer.
3. The first paragraph contains more than it should. The discussion of land development should be in a separate paragraph.	3. What should an opening paragraph do for the reader? Does this opening do that? What would you change?
4. The argument is sometimes weakened by sarcasm and by oversimplified reasons and examples.	4. How do you feel about the arguments in paragraphs 2 and 3? Do you think they strengthen or weaken the writer's position? Explain your answer.

Sentence Construction

Notes	Discussion Prompts
1. Run-on sentences are used (par. 1, 2, and 4).	1. Are there any run-on sentences or fragments? How would you change them?
2. The writer uses a variety of sentence forms, including those using questions, at appropriate times in the text.	2. Notice the variety of sentences. Do they carry out the intentions of the writer?
3. Paragraphs 2 and 3 give us sentences in which the ideas were probably clear to the writer but need more explanation to be clear to the reader.	3. In some sentences the meaning is not clear. It's as if the writer were in a hurry. Words may be missing or inexact. Can you find such sentences?

Usage

Notes	Discussion Prompts
1. Unless you're writing poetry, avoid rhyming words in a serious text (par. 1, sent. 1).	1. Read the first sentence aloud. What do you notice and how do you respond to that?
2. Word choice is not always accurate and causes confusion.	2. Considering the purpose of the letter and the audience, do you find any words that are either inaccurate or unsuitable? What would you change, add, or omit?
3. There is one homonym error (last par., sent. 2).	3. Can you find any homonym errors? What is the intended word?

Mechanics

Notes	Discussion Prompts
1. There are both internal and external punctuation errors.	1. Where do punctuation errors interfere with understanding?
2. Spelling errors appear.	2. Proofread for spelling.
3. There are some capitalization errors.	3. Do you capitalize Mother and Father in this situation? Explain. Are there any other questionable capital letters?

Prompt #5: Animal Rights

An animal rights group has asked you to join them to draft a Bill of Rights for Animals. The group believes that hunting rights, new land development that destroys animals' homes, and scientific experiments are a few of the things that have caused unnecessary suffering to animals and have endangered the existence of many species. Do you think animals are entitled to a bill of rights? What do you think the consequences of such a bill might be? Would you join the group?

Write a letter to the animal rights group stating your position about a Bill of Rights for Animals. Begin your letter with "Dear Members:" and tell them whether or not you will join them. Explain what you agree with or disagree with. Since your response could seriously affect the action this group takes, you want your position to be fully supported by logical reasoning and good examples.

Dear Members:

I would join your group. I think that animals should have the same rights as humans. People are killing animals left and right without thinking about it.

I think animals should have their own Bill of Rights. The Government should leave open areas like Parks and Reservations alone. They should let animals live in harmony. The animals don't harm us so we shouldn't harm them. I think that animals should be used for scientific experiments. If we don't use animals we won't find cures for such diseases as Aids and cancer. I think the Government should mark off places where people can hunt and places where people can't hunt.

I think it is terrible what these people are doing to those poor animals. Just the other day I was watching TV and they were saying eagles or some kind of bird in the eagle family was very close to extinction. People kill them and stuff them. That is really asham.

But one thing I have to disagree with you on. That's the part where you said something about scientific experiments. Well I really can't see anything wrong with that because they can't do these experiments on humans. I'm not saying that they should kill animals for simple tests like an antidope for a simple cold thats stupid. I also think it's stupid and cruel to test eye makeup and cosmetics on animals. That's wrong. But I do think they can put tests on animals for a cure for Aids or cancer that's helping us.

Unfortunately if the Government made a Bill for animal's Rights many people would become upset. Such people like hunters, building contractors, and scientists. The public might be upset because they won't be able to have new homes.

I would be happy to join your group, but I wouldn't want to go to far and upset the public.

Yours truly,
Mary Smith

Paper C

Notes	Discussion Prompts
Content/Organization	
1. The writer makes several points and attempts to support them with examples and reasons.	1. What are the main points of the paper? Does the writer support them?
2. The conclusion does not grow logically out of the paper. It contradicts the main argument.	2. How do you respond to the conclusion of this paper?
3. The writer uses too many first-person observations, which weaken the argument.	3. Try removing the first-person observations (*I think* phrases) in her paper. How does that affect the arguments?
4. The second paragraph lacks unity. There are no transitional words that link ideas together.	4. What are some of the problems with paragraph 2? Would transitional words help? Should some ideas be developed in separate paragraphs?
Sentence Construction	
1. Many ideas need to be combined to show their relationship to each other, to make more powerful statements, and to reduce wordiness (par. 1, sent. 1 and 2; par. 2, sent. 3 and 4; par. 3, sent. 4 and 5; par. 4, sent. 6, 7, and 8; par. 5, sent. 1 and 2).	1. Are there any ideas that could be combined into compound or complex sentences? Which ideas would you combine and why?
2. The writer uses run-on sentences and a fragment.	2. Correct the run-on sentences and the fragment.
Usage	
1. The writer uses an incorrect form of the verb *to be* (par. 1, sent. 1).	1. Is the word *would* being correctly used in the first sentence?
2. The writer's language is too casual and conversational for this occasion.	2. Who is the audience and what is the occasion for this letter? Is the language effective, appropriate? Which words or phrases would you change?
3. Vague and indefinite references (par. 3) are puzzling to the reader.	3. Who are these "people," and who are they in paragraph 3? Which words could you substitute to make the meaning clear?
4. There is a homonym error in the last paragraph.	4. Find the homonym error and choose the right word.
Mechanics	
1. There are several punctuation and capitalization errors that distract the reader.	1. Edit for punctuation and capitalization errors.
2. There are spelling errors.	2. Proofread for spelling errors.

Prompt #5: Animal Rights

An animal rights group has asked you to join them to draft a Bill of Rights for Animals. The group believes that hunting rights, new land development that destroys animals' homes, and scientific experiments are a few of the things that have caused unnecessary suffering to animals and have endangered the existence of many species. Do you think animals are entitled to a bill of rights? What do you think the consequences of such a bill might be? Would you join the group?

Write a letter to the animal rights group stating your position about a Bill of Rights for Animals. Begin your letter with "Dear Members:" and tell them whether or not you will join them. Explain what you agree with or disagree with. Since your response could seriously affect the action this group takes, you want your position to be fully supported by logical reasoning and good examples.

Dear Members

I received your letter. I'm a concerned citizen who objected to what you are doing to our animals.

There is know reason to hunt for game or develop land were the animal's live. But most of all, why do you need to make them suffer by doing crul tests on them. Know one can justify that crulity.

Animals have obligations too. Therefore they should be able to live in there own way. They to have familys to take care off.

If you build buildings, work constructions in aryas that there is no call for, then that is vilating there own homes.

When there were no more homes for them to settle down in, then what. They begin roming the streets.

To us, animals are entertainment. If there is no place provided for them, who knows what crisises may happen to endanger there lives.

Concerned Citizen

Paper J

Score **1**

Notes	Discussion Prompts
Content/Organization	
1. The writer has misread the question and blames the animal rights group for mistreating animals.	1. Does the writer understand the question?
2. The writer does not use paragraphs to develop ideas. In some places the paragraph has two or three ideas in it. In others, the writer starts a new paragraph with each sentence.	2. What's the problem with these paragraphs? How would you improve the paragraphing?
3. Ideas are so sparsely developed it's hard to understand what the writer had in mind.	3. Does the writer develop ideas sufficiently? Select two ideas in this paper and tell how you would develop them.
Sentence Construction	
1. Ideas need to be combined so the reader understands their relationship to each other.	1. How would you create more effective sentences showing the relationship between ideas?
2. Important connecting words in paragraph 4 are either missing or incorrect, making it difficult for the reader to follow the writer's ideas.	2. Reread the fourth paragraph. How would you change the construction of that sentence to make the meaning clear? What words would you add or change?
Usage	
1. Vague pronoun references (par. 4) create confusion.	1. If you haven't already eliminated the confusions in paragraph 4, pay attention to the pronoun references. Are they clear?
2. Homonym errors appear.	2. Correct homonym errors.
3. Formal letters require a complimentary closing.	3. This is a formal letter. What's missing?
4. Wrong verb tenses are used.	4. Why is it important for verb tenses to be accurate? Which verb tenses would you change for consistency and accuracy?
Mechanics	
1. There are internal as well as external punctuation errors.	1. Edit for punctuation.
2. The number of spelling errors makes the paper difficult to read.	2. Proofread for spelling.

General Question for the Whole Packet

Which papers taught you the most about sentence construction?

Prompt #6: Moral Dilemma

One of your closest friends has asked you to help him (or her) convince his parents that he was at your house when, in fact, he was at a party with other friends of whom his parents disapprove. Your friend is afraid his (or her) parents will punish him severely if they find out. Now you have a problem you must solve—how best to help your friend. Although you value the friendship, you are uncomfortable about what you have been asked to do, but you would like to be able to help your friend.

Write a letter telling your friend whether or not you have decided to help him (or her). In either case, support your decision with good reasons for your action and suggest a way to solve the problem that will improve your friend's relationship with his parents and not endanger your friendship with him.

Dear Mike:

I don't like what I'm doing because I really respect your parents, but I will help you so that you don't get severely punished. Although I disapprove of you hanging out with those kids because they have some bad habits, I want to help you because you are my friend and because you are in trouble.

I'm also willing to help you because I trust you, and I know that the other kids you went to the party with are basically nice. You and I went to elementary school together, so we've known each other for a long time, and we've been through a lot together. (I hope that nothing went on at the party that you didn't tell me about to make me regret I ever lied to your parents.)

As you know, I have great respect for your parents and for their decissions. I know you're angry at them now and probably saying, "These are my friends, and I can hang around with anybody I want," but you have to remember that I'm your friend, too, and I, like your parents, want what's best for you. Your parents don't approve of these kids because they haven't had the chance to find out what they're really like. They think these kids will be a bad influence on you. Maybe you can introduce some of them to your parents, so that they will be able to understand them better. Then you wouldn't have to lie to your parents about seeing your friends.

I'm uncomfortable because I don't approve of lying, even for a friend. However, I know how severe your parents can be (even though I like them), and, as a friend, I don't want you to be punished. In the future I'd like you to feel free to talk to me before you do anything like this again. Maybe we could figure out a better way to handle the situation. I'm sure you understand that I won't lie for you again, but that I'll always be your friend.

On your side,
Kevin

Paper O

Score 4

Notes	Discussion Prompts
Content/Organization	
1. Even as an informal letter to a friend, the composition is well organized and easy to follow. It has an opening paragraph, a midsection with reasons that explain the writer's decision, and a logical conclusion based on the argument.	1. Do you think this is a well-organized argument? Why?
2. The writer has several ideas to express and develops them in separate paragraphs.	2. Do the paragraphs help you understand the author's points?
3. Within the paragraphs, ideas are expressed in a logical sequence.	3. Do the ideas within a paragraph logically follow each other? Select a paragraph to illustrate.
4. Transitional words and deliberate repetition help to link ideas.	4. Which words does the writer use to help link ideas?
5. The content is well thought-out and reflects the writer's difficult situation. The reader senses the writer's honesty and his struggle to make a decision.	5. What adjectives would you use to describe the content? Explain.
Sentence Construction	
1. The writer has excellent control of sentences and knows how to combine ideas into mature and interesting statements (par. 1, sent. 1 and 2; par. 2, sent. 1 and 2; par. 3, sent. 2, 3, and 4; par. 4, sent. 2 and 4).	1. How does the writer combine ideas? What does he achieve by doing this?
2. Parallel structure helps to link ideas and create effective sentences (par. 1, sent. 2; par. 2, sent. 2; par. 3, sent. 1; par. 4, sent. 4).	2. Find an example of parallel structure and tell why it makes the sentence more effective.
3. The writer takes sentence risks to create a personal sound.	3. Which sentences make you interested in what the writer has to say? Explain why.
Usage	
1. Pronoun usage is sometimes ambiguous. Pronouns do not always clearly refer to antecedents and are sometimes used to refer to the same antecedent (par. 3).	1. Reread paragraph 3. Where do you find some confusion in the sentences? What causes the confusion and how would you clarify the ideas?
2. The possessive-case pronoun should be used in the second sentence of paragraph 1 because the writer doesn't disapprove of his friend but of his friend's "hanging out."	2. Does the word *you* in the second sentence of paragraph 1 really convey the author's meaning? Which word would be more accurate? Why?

Notes	Discussion Prompts
Usage, continued	
3. Word choice is good. The writer uses standard formal English as well as colloquial English, the latter of which is appropriate for an informal letter to a friend.	3. Who is the audience for this letter? Do you think the language is effective and appropriate?
Mechanics	
1. One error in spelling (par. 3, sent. 1) appears. 2. The writer knows how to use the comma in a variety of sentence situations.	1. Proofread the paper for spelling. 2. Proofread for punctuation. Explain the use of commas in the last paragraph.

Prompt #6: Moral Dilemma

One of your closest friends has asked you to help him (or her) convince his parents that he was at your house when, in fact, he was at a party with other friends of whom his parents disapprove. Your friend is afraid his (or her) parents will punish him severely if they find out. Now you have a problem you must solve—how best to help your friend. Although you value the friendship, you are uncomfortable about what you have been asked to do, but you would like to be able to help your friend.

Write a letter telling your friend whether or not you have decided to help him (or her). In either case, support your decision with good reasons for your action and suggest a way to solve the problem that will improve your friend's relationship with his parents and not endanger your friendship with him.

Dear Alice:

I'm very sorry but, I cannot lie to your parents. I think that if I do, I'll probably get myself into trouble for being dishonest. Consequently, I advise you to be honest with your parents also.I'm sure they have good reasons for disapproving your friends . I feel they are just doing this for your own safety.

I'm sure your friends are nice kids but, they are disapproved by your parents. Surely, if you talk with your parents and state your opinion on this matter, they might understand.

I am aware of the fact that you will be punished severely but, if you lie to your parents, they're sure to find out somehow, and this will just increase your chance of getting an even more severe punishment.

By lying to your parents, they will no longer trust you. Also, they will find out I lied, and they might not trust me to be a good friend to you.

I don't think I'm being a good friend if I let you get into trouble and,possibly, danger. I also don't think you're a very good friend if you want me to lie to your parents and you go to a party with those kind of friends.

I apologise if my decision does not please you. Please try to understand.

Your friend,
Nancy

Paper Q

Notes	Discussion Prompts
Content/Organization	

Notes	Discussion Prompts
1. The writer has a sense of organization. The paper has a beginning statement, followed by several ideas and an ending.	1. Is the paper well organized? Does the conclusion logically follow the writer's ideas?
2. Although the writer has many good ideas, the paragraphs are not developed with enough examples or facts. The letter reads more like an outline than a full expression.	2. Are the paragraphs developed enough to satisfy you? Would you like more information?
3. Paragraphs need to have some transitional words or phrases so that a reader can see how one idea connects to another.	3. Do the ideas flow easily from one paragraph to another? What could you add?

Sentence Construction

Notes	Discussion Prompts
1. Sentences in paragraph 1 need to be combined to avoid choppiness and to show the logical relationship between ideas.	1. To avoid short, choppy sentences, where could you combine ideas into logical and more interesting sentences?
2. Faulty coordination strings clauses together with *and* or *but* when they should be subordinated.	2. *And* and *but* are coordinating conjunctions and shouldn't be used to combine ideas in situations where one idea is subordinate to another. Check each use of these conjunctions and replace them where necessary with a more accurate conjunction.
3. A dangling participle confuses the reader (par. 4).	3. Look at the first sentence in paragraph 4. It doesn't really make sense. Who is "lying to your parents"? Not *they*. How would you correct this?

Usage

Notes	Discussion Prompts
1. *Disapprove* is part of an idiomatic expression that takes the pronoun *of* (par. 1 and 2).	1. What is an idiom? Can you find an example of an idiomatic phrase? Is it correctly written?
2. An adjective must agree in number with the noun it modifies (par. 5).	2. What's the mistake in a phrase like "those kind of friends"? How would you correct it?
3. Because the choice of words is sometimes too formal for the audience and the occasion, the tone of the letter sounds insincere and cold.	3. Who is the audience for this letter? What is your response to the writer's choice of words?

Mechanics

Notes	Discussion Prompts
1. Commas should precede, not follow, the coordinating conjunction.	1. Are commas used correctly?
2. One spelling error occurs.	2. Proofread for spelling errors.

Paper F

Prompt #6: Moral Dilemma

One of your closest friends has asked you to help him (or her) convince his parents that he was at your house when, in fact, he was at a party with other friends of whom his parents disapprove. Your friend is afraid his (or her) parents will punish him severely if they find out. Now you have a problem you must solve—how best to help your friend. Although you value the friendship, you are uncomfortable about what you have been asked to do, but you would like to be able to help your friend.

Write a letter telling your friend whether or not you have decided to help him (or her). In either case, support your decision with good reasons for your action and suggest a way to solve the problem that will improve your friend's relationship with his parents and not endanger your friendship with him.

Dear Joe:

The kids that you hang out with, are probably nice kids. But smoking is a very serious problem. They might talk you into smoking. Or if some of them are not interested in school they might talk you into cutting school too. If you get caught then you will get in very deep trouble, and I won't be able to help you.

It is probably none of my business, and I think those kids could do very terrible things and I don't think you should get in trouble because of them. Alot of kids are like that, when you get in trouble, they don't care what happens to you. That's why I think you should listen to your parents. They probably understand alot more about these kids then you do. The fact that you have to lie to your parents is terrible too.

Your parents probably will find out one way or another and I could get in trouble too. I don't want to get involved in this. What you do is your business, and I don't want to keep lying for you. It makes me feel terrible too.

This is the first, and the last time I am going to do this. I hope my fears never come true, but if anything ever does happen, don't say I didn't warn you.

Your friend,
Ralph

Paper F

Teacher's Guide, Prompt #6

Notes	Discussion Prompts
Content/Organization	

Notes	Discussion Prompts
1. The letter needs an opening paragraph which states the problem and the author's position. Paragraph 1 is part of the argument, not an opening statement.	1. Does the paper have a good opening? Why or why not?
2. The paragraphs lack unity. Some sentences are either unsupported or unrelated to the main idea of the paragraph.	2. What do we mean by "paragraph unity"? Examine each of the paragraphs to see if they are unified.
3. The writer has a sense of organization and offers several ideas that lead to a conclusion based on the argument.	3. Even though there are problems in this paper, there are still good things about it. List three good points about the content and organization.

Sentence Construction

Notes	Discussion Prompts
1. Short, separate sentences need to be combined into more interesting sentences that show the relationship between ideas.	1. In some places, do you have trouble connecting the ideas between one sentence and another? Try combining some of the shorter sentences into longer and more interesting ones that show the reader the relationships between ideas.
2. A run-on sentence and fragments are used.	2. Proofread for complete sentences.
3. Sentences are often loosely strung together with *and*.	3. Examine the use of *and* in these sentences. Is it always correctly used? Choose a more accurate conjunction wherever it seems necessary.

Usage

Notes	Discussion Prompts
1. The word *then* is incorrectly used instead of *than* (par. 2, sent. 4).	1. *Then* and *than* are homonyms. What is the difference in meaning? Which one should be used in paragraph 2, sentence 4?
2. A colloquial level of usage is appropriate in a letter to a friend.	2. How would you describe the tone of this letter? What is your response to the writer's vocabulary?

Mechanics

Notes	Discussion Prompts
1. Commas are sometimes misplaced or have been omitted.	1. Edit for commas and explain your reasons for adding or deleting any of them.
2. Spelling is correct except for one consistent error (*alot*, par. 2).	2. Proofread for spelling.

Prompt #6: Moral Dilemma

One of your closest friends has asked you to help him (or her) convince his parents that he was at your house when, in fact, he was at a party with other friends of whom his parents disapprove. Your friend is afraid his (or her) parents will punish him severely if they find out. Now you have a problem you must solve—how best to help your friend. Although you value the friendship, you are uncomfortable about what you have been asked to do, but you would like to be able to help your friend.

Write a letter telling your friend whether or not you have decided to help him (or her). In either case, support your decision with good reasons for your action and suggest a way to solve the problem that will improve your friend's relationship with his parents and not endanger your friendship with him.

Dear Jim:

I refuse to tell your parents you were at my house, when you really went to a party. What you did was wrong and uncalled for. You didn't invite me to the party, which is allright. I didn't want to go anyways. I can take a hint you didn't want me around. You didn't invite me and you want me to cover up for you. I know you would cover up for me, too. This time I just can't do it. If your parents find out, they would give you a bigger punishment and they would tell my parents. Then we would both get punished. I also want you to learn a little responsebility. You need to take things seriousley in your life. If you ever think I'm doing this, because you didn't invite me you're wrong. I didn't want to go. I still want to be your best friend. Don't take this as if I don't want to be your best friend. You did something wrong, so you have to face what happens. You will get punished, but then your punishment won't last forever. You did something behind your parents back without them knowing. Some children don't have parents. Don't take advantage of what you have that other people didn't have. You should tell your parents, straight up, that what you did was wrong and you will take the punishment. I know you think I'm crazy but you will thank me for writing this letter to you. You shouldn't have been hanging around with those other children. They smoke and don't like school. You are different from them. If you keep on hanging around people like that, you're libal to end up like them. I can't imagine you as a person who doesn't like school and started smoking. Take advise from a friend, before your life comes to an end.

Paper A

Score **1**

Notes	Discussion Prompts
Content/Organization	
1. The student is not forming an argument so much as rambling. Ideas are introduced at random without any attempt to develop them into separate paragraphs logically connected to each other.	1. How many different paragraphs can you find in this paper? What ideas, reasons, or examples might you use to develop them?
2. Letter form requires a complimentary closing and a signature.	2. As a letter, this paper needs to follow a special form. What needs to be included?
3. The reader feels a lack of sincerity because the writer's advice seems so glib and because the reader suspects the writer is really angry at not being invited to the party. The statements contradict each other.	3. What is your response to the content of this paper?
Sentence Construction	
1. Sentences lack variety. There are too many short declarative sentences that could have been combined into more interesting statements.	1. Does the writer use a variety of sentence constructions? What would you change and why?
2. The writer uses the wrong conjunction in a clause (sent. 6) that should be contrasted with the preceding idea, not coordinated with it.	2. Is the conjunction *and* being used correctly in the sixth sentence?
3. The rhymed last line is inappropriate in a serious piece of writing.	3. What's your response to the last sentence? Would you change any words?
4. Sequence of tenses is often incorrect.	4. Proofread the paper for correct verb tenses. Where do you find problems? What tense would you use and why?
Usage	
1. Two vocabulary words are incorrect. *Uncalled for* (sent. 3) is a poor word choice, and there's no such word as *anyways* (sent. 4).	1. Is the writer's word choice accurate, effective, appropriate? Are there any words you would change? Explain.
2. The pronoun *them* is incorrectly used (sent. 19).	2. Which word in this sentence sounds incorrect to you: "You did something behind your parents back without them knowing it." What would you say and why?
Mechanics	
1. Several spelling errors occur.	1. Proofread for spelling.
2. Punctuation errors with commas and an apostrophe occur.	2. Edit for punctuation.
General Question for the Whole Packet	

Which paper best demonstrates the importance of tone? Explain.

Appendix

Using a Six-Point Scale

Some teachers may wish to use a six-point scoring scale, which is the scale most state assessments use. This appendix contains a Six-Point Master Rubric and a student Holistic Scoring Guide using a six-point scale. It also contains two additional essays for each of the six prompts presented in the second section of this book; a Teacher's Guide for each essay is provided. This appendix also contains a revised scoring for the essays in the second section so that they fit into the six-point scale.

Using essay packets for a six-point scale is similar to using them for a four-point scale. The revised teaching tips in this section of the book will help you organize your lesson plan for using these packets.

A Guide to the Model Essays, Using the Six-Point Scale

Prompt Topic/page on which prompt appears	Essay Letter	Score on Six-Point Scale	Page Number for Essay	Page Number for Discussion Prompts
Someone Important				
42	T	6	45	46
	X	5	47	48
	V	4	49	50
	S	3	52	53
	W	2	103	104
	U	1	105	106
Writing a Story				
42	D	6	54	55
	Y	5	56	57
	G	4	58	59
	Z	3	60	61
	C	2	107	108
	B	1	109	110
School Video				
43	W	6	62	63
	E	5	111	112
	L	4	64	65
	N	3	66	67
	H	2	68	69
	O	1	113	114
Problem at Your School				
43	M	6	71	72
	Y	5	115	116
	R	4	73	74
	E	3	76	77
	B	2	78	79
	D	1	118	119
Animal Rights				
44	G	6	120	122
	K	5	81	82
	I	4	83	84
	C	3	85	86
	H	2	123	124
	J	1	87	88
Moral Dilemma				
44	M	6	125	126
	O	5	89	90
	Q	4	92	93
	F	3	94	95
	A	2	96	97
	P	1	127	128

Holistic Scoring Guide for Students

Before beginning to score papers, follow these rules:

1. Read all six papers in the set before scoring any one of them.
2. Remember that the best papers aren't necessarily perfect, and the weakest papers can still make good points.
3. Read the whole paper before you score it. Here are some guidelines to help you decide on the score.

Score This is the best paper in the set as far as content and organization are concerned. The paper has few, if any, problems with sentences. Vocabulary is appropriate and effective, and there are very few, if any, problems with grammar or mechanics. You will probably answer "yes" to almost all of the questions on the Writing Checklist.

Score 5 This is also a good paper. The content is interesting and the paper is well organized. There may be some errors in paragraphing and in sentence structure, but basically, this person writes well with few errors in grammar or mechanics.

Score 4 This is still one of the better papers. Although some of the ideas may not have been fully developed, the content is still engaging and the writer's voice is still strong. However, there are more sentence errors. Word choice may not always be accurate or appropriate. Grammar errors begin to show up, as do mistakes in spelling and punctuation.

Score 3 You can see a real difference in content and the development of ideas between this paper and the better papers. Sentences often lack variety and may be more difficult to understand. There may also be errors in grammar and mechanics.

Score This paper has serious writing problems. There isn't very much content, and what is there has not been developed. There may not be an opening or a satisfying conclusion. Sentence errors as well as problems with grammar and mechanics appear. The writer may lack a sense of audience and purpose.

Score The writer has a very difficult time expressing himself or herself. There's very little content and probably no understanding of paragraphing. The writer also has trouble with sentence construction. Poor spelling and grammar mistakes also make it hard for the reader to understand the writer. On your Writing Checklist, you will probably answer "no" most often to questions about this paper.

Six-Point Master Rubric

Score 6	Score 5	Score 4	Score 3	Score 2	Score 1
The writer has a strong grasp of written language.	*The writer has a good command of written language.*	*This paper is good, but it lacks development in some areas and is stylistically ineffective at some points.*	*This paper has decent content, but overall it uses written language poorly.*	*This paper shows that the writer has limited skill in written expression.*	*The writer lacks control of written expression.*

Content/Organization

Score 6	Score 5	Score 4	Score 3	Score 2	Score 1
• Is organized effectively around a single focus • Includes appropriate details, examples and reasons • Moves logically from opening to closing • Demonstrates analytical, critical, and/or creative thinking • Contains interesting and original ideas • Contains unified, well-developed paragraphs with fluent transitions between ideas	• Is organized around a single focus • Develops one idea in each paragraph • Includes some details, examples, or reasons • Moves logically from opening to conclusion	• Is organized effectively • Develops one idea in each paragraph • Includes few details, examples, reasons • Leaves room for fuller development or more effective presentation of ideas	• Attempts to develop a main idea, but paragraphs do not have enough details, examples, and reasons • Separates ideas that belong together into different paragraphs • Lacks transitions between paragraphs and ideas • May lack a beginning, a middle, or an ending	• Attempts to develop a main idea, but paragraphs do not have relevant details, examples, or reasons • Lacks clear organization • Paragraphs lack unity • Lacks transitions • Lacks a beginning, a middle, or an ending	• Does not develop a main idea • Lacks a beginning, a middle, or an ending • Does not use paragraphs • Does not communicate purpose clearly

Sentence Construction

Score 6	Score 5	Score 4	Score 3	Score 2	Score 1
• Uses a variety of sentence structures effectively • Contains few, if any, errors in sentence construction • Uses sophisticated devices (such as dependent clauses, appositives,	• May contain errors in sentence construction	• Contains syntactical errors, such as shifts in simple subjects, dangling modifiers, run-ons and fragments	• Lacks sentence variety • Contains syntactical errors	• Lacks sentence variety • Contains frequent syntactical errors, such as run-ons, fragments, shifts in subject, and overuse of word *and*	• Contains frequent syntactical errors, such as run-ons, fragments, shifts in subject, and overuse of word *and* • Contains incoherent sentences, sometimes because

continued on next page

Score 6	Score 5	Score 4	Score 3	Score 2	Score 1
Sentence Construction, continued					
and parallel structure) to show relationships between ideas					important connecting words are missing or used incorrectly • Includes short, choppy sentences and/or long, rambling ones
Usage					
• Contains few, if any, errors in grammar • Uses appropriate language for audience and purpose of piece	• Shows an awareness of audience and purpose • Demonstrates good command of language although errors in grammar may appear, usually with pronouns	• Contains grammar errors, especially with pronoun agreement and pronoun reference • Includes ineffective word choice	• Contains errors in grammar • Contains ineffective or inappropriate word choice	• Contains grammar errors • Contains some usage problems, such as homonym errors • Includes inexact or inappropriate word choice	• Contains significant usage problems such as subject-verb agreement, pronoun use, and word choice • Includes inappropriate word choice
Mechanics					
• Includes few, if any, errors in mechanics	• Contains relatively few errors in spelling, capitalization, and punctuation	• Contains mistakes in spelling and punctuation that don't interfere with reading	• May contain some mechanical errors	• Includes many mechanical errors that distract the reader	• Includes many mechanical errors that interfere with the reader's understanding

Prompt #1: Someone Important

Think about someone who plays a special part in your life. This person could be a member of your family, a friend, or a neighbor—someone who might have done something important for you, or someone you just like to be with. If you were writing your autobiography, this person would have his or her own chapter.

Imagine writing your life story and write a chapter about this person. Tell what the relationship is between you and why it is special. Tell about one or two different experiences you have had together to show why the relationship is so important to you. Be sure to describe this person.

The person that is special to me is not a person, it is my dog Casey.

When I have to go to school on Monday after we played all weekend he will come into my bed and lik my face.

Casey is a golden Retreever he is 10 years old, his tail wags in your face and tikles you he is very funny.

He was sick last year I was scared they would put him to sleep he has been in our family since he was a puppy.

I don't know how I could live without him he is my Best Friend.

Score **2**

Teacher's Guide, Prompt #1

Notes	Discussion Prompts
Content/Organization	

Notes	Discussion Prompts
1. The writer has a sense of how to organize a paper into a beginning, a middle, and an end. Each section of the paper, however, needs to be developed.	1. Does this opening paragraph interest you, make you want to read on? How would you rewrite it?
2. Paragraphs 2 and 3 could be combined and developed, starting with a good topic sentence.	2. What ideas could be included and developed in the same paragraph? Write a topic sentence that would cover both stories. What else might you add to this paragraph?
3. The paragraph about the dog being sick could have more details.	3. What questions could you ask the writer about the time the dog was sick? What could you then add to the paragraph? Are there any other questions you would ask the writer to help him or her develop the essay?

Sentence Construction

Notes	Discussion Prompts
1. The writer does not have a command of sentence structure.	1. Edit for run-on sentences or fragments. Try to combine related ideas into compound or complex sentences.
2. In paragraph 3 there's a shift in sentence construction from the author's point of view to the reader's, from third person to second person.	2. Besides being a run-on sentence, what else is wrong with the sentence in paragraph 3? How would you correct this other sentence-construction error?

Usage

Notes	Discussion Prompts
1. The pronouns *that* and *it* are questionable in the opening sentence since both refer to the noun *person.*	1. Do you think the first sentence is grammatically correct? Explain.
2. Avoid general and vague pronoun references like *they* (par. 4).	2. Who is *they* in the sentence about Casey's being put to sleep? What would be a better word?

Mechanics

Notes	Discussion Prompts
1. There are several spelling mistakes.	1. Proofread for spelling.
2. Breeds of animals are not capitalized unless the name includes a country (French poodle). Best Friend is worth discussing.	2. Are all the capital letters necessary?
3. Two commas are needed.	3. Can you find the places where a comma should be used? Explain.

Prompt #1: Someone Important

Think about someone who plays a special part in your life. This person could be a member of your family, a friend, or a neighbor—someone who might have done something important for you, or someone you just like to be with. If you were writing your autobiography, this person would have his or her own chapter.

Imagine writing your life story and write a chapter about this person. Tell what the relationship is between you and why it is special. Tell about one or two different experiences you have had together to show why the relationship is so important to you. Be sure to describe this person.

This person is special. I will describe this person. This person has brown hair. It is a girl. She is nice and my best friend. She has very long hair. Her favorite food is chocolate. She is a good athlete and great at soccer. The position this person plays is defense. Two good experiences we have had together one is when we went to the pool and we played. Another is when she came to my house for lunch.

Score | 1 |

Paper U

Notes	Discussion Prompts

Content/Organization

Notes	Discussion Prompts
1. The writer has very little experience with written text. The content lacks interest. It almost reads as if the writer were answering test questions about the subject.	1. What is your response to the content of this paper?
2. The major problem here is lack of content and no understanding of how to organize written text.	2. How would you help this beginning writer? What would you tell the writer first about organizing a paper?
3. There is no development of any idea.	3. How would you divide this paper into paragraphs? What might be a topic sentence for each paragraph?

Sentence Construction

Notes	Discussion Prompts
1. The simple sentence pattern is boring. Ideas can be combined. There are even possibilities for question or exclamation marks.	1. How could you provide variety for these sentences?
2. The next-to-last sentence is a run-on sentence.	2. Proofread for run-on sentences and fragments.

Usage

Notes	Discussion Prompts
1. The writer's vocabulary is limited, and the repetition of the phrase *this person* weakens the paper.	1. What's your response to the writer's vocabulary? Are the words correct, effective, and appropriate? Select at least one place to substitute a more vivid choice of words.
2. *It* can't be used as a pronoun to refer to people (sent. 4).	2. Is the writer's grammar correct throughout?

Mechanics

Notes	Discussion Prompts
1. There are no errors in mechanics. The main problem with this paper is the lack of content.	1. Proofread for spelling and punctuation.

Prompt #2: Writing a Story

Your class is collecting stories for a book to be published by the end of the year. The editors will pick two stories written from the same opening sentence. Using the following opening sentence, let your imagination lead you into a story: "Sally looked out the window and saw the person she dreaded most coming up the front steps."

To be considered, your story should have a beginning, a middle, and an ending. It should include description as well as dialogue. But most of all, it should be interesting and have some original ideas in it.

The morning was very bright and sunny. Sally suddenly saw the evil shadow. Who killed her best friend Sam were back! Only Sally could see the shadow. Her Mother didnt even know they were here. They didn't bother to knock on the door they walked right trough the door. Just as the shadow was about to grab Sally a cloud came out and coverd the sun. "I'll get you next time," said the shadow as he disapeard. The next morning when the sun came out again so did the shadow. Sally was to fritend to move. Just then her friend Sam came back from the dead. The shadow and Sam faght, it was a feerce fight. They both used there magical powers. Her friend Sam won and asked Sally to come back with him but she couldnt.

Paper C

Notes	Discussion Prompts
Content/Organization	
1. The writer doesn't use paragraphs to organize ideas.	1. How would you organize this paper?
2. The content lacks sufficient information to tell a complete story.	2. Does the story have enough information? What questions would you ask the writer?
Sentence Construction	
1. There are two run-on sentences and a fragment.	1. Edit for run-on sentences and sentence fragments.
Usage	
1. There are agreement problems between a singular subject and a plural verb (sent. 3) and between a singular subject and a plural pronoun (sent. 5 and 6).	1. Were there any grammar errors? Explain your answer.
2. Two homonym errors need correction.	2. Are there any homonym errors?
Mechanics	
1. There are spelling errors.	1. Proofread for spelling.
2. Commas are needed for various reasons.	2. Where would you place commas? Explain your reasons.
3. *Mother* doesn't need a capital letter.	3. Are capital letters correct?
4. Apostrophes are needed in two contractions (sent. 5 and last sent.).	4. Proofread for all other punctuation.

Paper B

Prompt #2: Writing a Story

Your class is collecting stories for a book to be published by the end of the year. The editors will pick two stories written from the same opening sentence. Using the following opening sentence, let your imagination lead you into a story: "Sally looked out the window and saw the person she dreaded most coming up the front steps."

To be considered, your story should have a beginning, a middle, and an ending. It should include description as well as dialogue. But most of all, it should be interesting and have some original ideas in it.

It was Mr. Weerd the Princabul. Oh no what does he want here. So Sally pertend not to look at him. Hello Mr. Weerd how are you doing asked Sally Mom. And they talked in anoter room for an our and Sally was afrad they was talking about her and she was very glad wen he left.

Paper B

Teacher's Guide, Prompt #2

Notes	Discussion Prompts
Content/Organization	
1. There is so little content here that it's difficult to understand what the point of the story is. This is the work of a very inexperienced writer.	1. If you were trying to help this writer really get into the subject, what questions would you ask?
2. Even given these few sentences, the story could be organized into paragraphs.	2. How does the story divide into paragraphs?
Sentence Construction	
1. The writer has a poor idea of sentence structure and runs ideas together using the word *and*.	1. Edit the run-on sentences into logical sentence units. They need not be simple sentences, and you may use whatever words you need to connect the ideas.
Usage	
1. There is one error in grammar, a subject-verb agreement (last sent.).	1. Proofread for correct grammar.
Mechanics	
1. The writer doesn't use the space of the line.	1. What is your response to the way the story looks on the paper? What should it look like?
2. There are many errors in spelling.	2. Proofread for spelling errors.
3. Punctuation is a problem.	3. Ignoring the run-on sentences, which you have already revised, what other punctuation problems need attention?
4. Two words (*Princabul* and *Mom*) are capitalized that don't need to be.	4. Proofread for capitalization.

Prompt #3: School Video

Your class has decided to make a 15-minute video about your school. The purpose of the video is to show the parents of new students the best things about the school.

Write a presentation to your class in which you include a statement of what you hope to achieve with this movie. Select three things about the school that you would highlight in the video and explain why.

Lincoln Middle School is a great place for me and my peers to come and learn. The teachers all have a wonderful personality as well as the students, office staff and other people committed to making this school fun and educational.

My first stop in the video is the office with Mr. Dean, the assistant principle, and Dr. Markov, the principle, who works extremely hard. Then there's our guidance counceler who makes sure that every student is doing well and has a smile on their face when they walk by his office.

The teachers are one of the most important people that make Lincoln such a good school. They teach subjects from Language to Spanish. They are always there for the students, talking and listening carefully to our questions and problems. They are very friendly, they'll wave and say hello in the hallway, and never raise their voices. If anyone at Lincoln deserves a pat on the back it is the teachers!

The most major thing that makes Lincoln a truly great school are the students. My friends are what gets me up in the morning, their smiling faces and positive attitudes greet me when I come to school. The students here are very bright and friendly. Their are only about two in a hundred kids that are trouble makers, and those who are, learn their lesson quickly after a couple of detentions. Many of the students here make the regular honeroll or distinguished honeroll. This is quite difficult because you have to get all "A's" and "B's" for the regular honeroll and all "A's" for the distinguished honeroll! At the end of the year honeroll students are rewarded with a special luncheon in the cafeteria.

There are lots of after school activities where you can meet friends and have fun. My video would take you to the Spanish Club and the French Club. These clubs take you on trips and have big parties on the holidays. Theirs an Arts and Crafts Club, Drama Club, and Golf Club. Just to mention a few.

We have wonderful teachers and students. Around twenty clubs and activities. Awesome music and sports programs. We hope that this video will show parents and new students what a great environment for learning Lincoln Middle School is.

Paper E

Score 5

Notes	Discussion Prompts
Content/Organization	
1. The paper is well organized in terms of a beginning, a middle, and an ending. Although the writer says Lincoln Middle School is a great place to learn, the emphasis is on the fun.	1. Are all the ideas in the opening paragraph developed in the paper?
2. The writer gives good details to support his or her ideas.	2. How does the writer develop his or her ideas?
3. The ending paragraph, however, is weak. It refers to music and sports programs that are never discussed in the paper. As a summary paragraph, it falls short of the material.	3. Do you think the last paragraph is effective? Explain.
Sentence Construction	
1. Although the writer does combine many ideas into complex sentences, he or she also has several fragments and run-on sentences.	1. Proofread for complete sentences.
Usage	
1. There are several agreement problems between singular and plural references and between a singular noun and a plural verb.	1. Find the grammar errors in each of the first four paragraphs. What kinds of errors are they? How would you correct them?
2. Sometimes the word choice is redundant, inaccurate, or cliché.	2. Do you think the writer's choice of words is accurate and effective? Would you make any changes?
3. There are homonym errors.	3. What are the homonym errors?
Mechanics	
1. There are spelling errors.	1. Proofread for spelling.
2. The writer makes several errors in the use of commas.	2. Proofread for correct comma placement.

Prompt #3: School Video

Your class has decided to make a 15-minute video about your school. The purpose of the video is to show the parents of new students the best things about the school.

Write a presentation to your class in which you include a statement of what you hope to achieve with this movie. Select three things about the school that you would highlight in the video and explain why.

Lincoln is a good place to go to. If you ever get hurt you still can get to class, withe elvator. All of the classes are easy to find. The teachers are nice. They teach us alot of new stuff. This school has many clubs here at Lincoln. Few clubs are the Spanish French and Crafts. At Lincoln sports here are football, restling, and baseball. Subjects taught here are science math geogerphy artes and many more. Doing this I hope I acheve in graduating from Lincoln.

Paper O

Notes	Discussion Prompts
Content/Organization	
1. The writer does not know how to organize ideas into paragraphs.	1. There are ideas here even though the writer has not organized them into paragraphs. How many possible paragraphs can you find?
2. Ideas are only stated, not developed.	2. What questions would you ask the writer to help him or her develop these ideas?
Sentence Construction	
1. Several sentences are cluttered with phrases that add nothing to the idea but simply repeat it. The word order can also be changed to increase interest in the sentences.	1. Pick two or three sentences that you could revise more effectively. What would you do?
Usage	
1. The writer creates a vagueness with the use of the indefinite pronoun *this* in the last sentence.	1. What's the problem with using the pronoun *this* in the last sentence?
2. The last sentence is unintelligible. The words may be in the writer's head, but they are not on the page.	2. Examine the last sentence. The choice of words at the end of the sentence is ungrammatical. There are also words missing, so the meaning is incomplete. What do you think the writer is trying to say?
Mechanics	
1. The writer has probably not proofread the paper because some of the errors are just the simple omission of connecting words or a dropped letter. Other words, of course, are obviously misspelled.	1. Proofread for spelling and for what is probably careless proofreading.

Paper Y

Prompt #4: Problem at Your School

You have been asked to serve on a school committee made up of parents, students, and teachers. The purpose of the committee is to identify and help solve the major problems in your school. The problems may involve classes, report cards, extracurricular activities, clubs, even the building itself. From your point of view as a student, select what you think is a serious problem facing your school today. Explain why you think it is important to solve this problem and tell how you would solve it.

Write a report to the school committee describing the problem and explaining why it must be solved if the school is to improve. Propose your solution to the problem, in an effort to convince the committee that your recommendations will improve the school.

If you walk around our school, you will see security guards patroling the hallways making sure things are okay. Theft is a big problem in our schools even though we've hired people to protect us from robbery.

I can think of a number of ways to stop theft in our school. First of all, the school must fix all of its old or broken lockers. I had a friend who had her whole soccer uniform (including expensive shoes) stolen right out of her locker because it wasn't closed correctly. Built-in locks should be taken off the lockers, and students should be allowed to bring in their own locks. This way, if the wrong person knows your combination, you can easily change the lock. Wouldn't it be easier to get our own locks? It would save the school money and time.

Another way to cut down on theft is having security guards inside the gym locker room while people are changing, and when nobody is changing, the door should be locked. Nobody should be allowed to enter the locker room before or after school hours. This would stop lots of thefts because many of my friends have had their lockers and gym clothes stolen. If this action took place, the amount of stealing will lower considerably. Before a person commits a crime, they must think of the consequences. The bigger the consequence is, the less likely it is that the person will commit the crime. If the authorities in school were to make the punishment for theft stronger, people would probably not risk stealing. The penalty for stealing should be either suspension, or having the person expelled.

These three steps would almost eliminate our theft problems. I propose that we do this without further delay and make our school a safer place.

Paper Y

Score 5

Notes	Discussion Prompts
Content/Organization	
1. The writer has thought carefully about a serious problem and offers a serious remedy. The writer suggests and develops several ideas.	1. How well does the writer answer the question?
2. The paper is well organized. It begins by involving the reader immediately in the scene and then stating the problem. Each paragraph takes up a new idea.	2. What do we mean by a "well-organized" paper? Is this paper well organized?
3. Although the writer has a good sense of paragraph unity, sentence 1 in paragraph 2 is better as part of the opening statement.	3. Is each paragraph unified? How do unified paragraphs help us to understand the paper?
4. Good transitions between ideas make the essay easy to follow.	4. How do transitional words or phrases help the reader? Can you find examples in this paper?
Sentence Construction	
1. The writer uses a variety of sentences and knows how to combine ideas effectively.	1. Find examples of different kinds of sentence structures. Why does the writer use them, and what effect do they have on the reader?
2. The dependent clause should come before the main clause (par. 1, sent. 2).	2. There are the two clauses in paragraph 1, sentence 2. Which should come first? Why?
3. Sentences need parallel structure.	3. Where would the paper profit from the use of parallel construction?
4. Faulty logic confuses the reader (par. 3, sent. 3).	4. Sentences have to be logical. Do you have any problems with the internal logic of any sentences? Can you correct the problem?
5. Unnecessary shifts in person and inexact verb tense (par. 2) confuse the reader.	5. Some sentences in paragraph 2 are hard to understand. Did you find any problems? How would you clarify the meaning?
Usage	
1. Although the writer generally demonstrates a good command of language and sentence structure, in some instances, the words are either inexact or too colloquial for the occasion.	1. Who is the audience and what is the purpose of this paper? Is the word choice appropriate? Would you change any words?
2. Indefinite pronoun references introduce vagueness (par. 3).	2. Compare the two uses of the word *this* in paragraph 3. Do you see a problem in either case? Explain. How would you alter the sentence?

Notes	Discussion Prompts
Usage, continued	
3. The pronoun must agree with its antecedent (par. 4, sent. 1).	3. Are there any errors in grammar?
Mechanics	
1. There is only one error in punctuation (par. 4, last sent.). 2. There is only one spelling error (*patroling*, in the first sent.).	1. Examine the punctuation. Are there any errors or problems? Explain your answer. 2. Proofread for spelling and correct any errors.

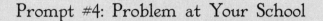

Paper D

Prompt #4: Problem at Your School

You have been asked to serve on a school committee made up of parents, students, and teachers. The purpose of the committee is to identify and help solve the major problems in your school. The problems may involve classes, report cards, extracurricular activities, clubs, even the building itself. From your point of view as a student, select what you think is a serious problem facing your school today. Explain why you think it is important to solve this problem and tell how you would solve it.

Write a report to the school committee describing the problem and explaining why it must be solved if the school is to improve. Propose your solution to the problem, in an effort to convince the committee that your recommendations will improve the school.

What is one of the problems of my school?
One of the problems that occurrs at this school are when there is one or
 even a couple children in a class disrupting the class in all kinds of ways doing all kinds of things. I have been in classes like this. I have
experience these annoying situations. The teacher don't really do anything about these children. If the teacher don't care about this the
children will keep on bothering and disrupting the class. There is one
 boy in my Gym class who I am just plainly afriad of. He always goes around hitting on my friends and me for no reason. I personly think
 that, that boy needs some phsycologicl help.
In conclusion I say that teachers need to pay more attention to how these children act in class and effect other people.

Paper D

Teacher's Guide, Prompt #4

Notes	Discussion Prompts
Content/Organization	
1. The writer states a problem but has not developed it with enough examples and facts. The solution to the problem is only a vague suggestion.	1. Given the problem this writer has posed, what facts and examples would you give to support it?
2. The attempt to organize the paper into a beginning, a middle, and an ending is weak. The first sentence is not really an opening; it simply repeats the assignment. In the same way, the last sentence isn't a conclusion but a repeat of the argument, offering the reader no further insights.	2. Why is the first sentence a weak opening and the last sentence a weak conclusion?
3. The writer doesn't have a grasp of paragraph structure and doesn't know how to indent.	3. What advice would you give this writer about paragraphing?
Sentence Construction	
1. An adverbial clause should not act as the predicate following the verb *to be* (sent. 2).	1. Find an example of a "when" clause following the verb *to be*. How is the meaning affected by this kind of sentence construction? How could you change the sentence?
2. Ideas need to be combined into more interesting sentences that show the relationship of one to another.	2. What do you see as a major problem with the sentences in paragraph 2? How could you make the sentence constructions more interesting?
Usage	
1. In paragraph 2, subject and verb must agree in number. Pronoun and antecedent must agree in number. The past participle form of the verb *experience* is needed.	1. Examine paragraph 2 for grammar errors. What kinds of errors do you find and how would you correct them?
2. Idiomatic use of the preposition *of* is required (sent. 2).	2. The phrase *a couple children* is incorrect. What is required? Explain.
3. Substandard usage weakens the paper.	3. Find an example of substandard vocabulary and replace it with more appropriate words for the intended audience.
Mechanics	
1. Incorrect hyphenating makes reading very difficult.	1. Which words should not be hyphenated? Hyphenate any others correctly.
2. Spelling errors distract the reader. There is also an error in capitalization.	2. Why are correct spelling, capitalization, and punctuation important conventions? Proofread this paper for those errors and correct them.

Prompt #5: Animal Rights

An animal rights group has asked you to join them to draft a Bill of Rights for Animals. The group believes that hunting rights, new land development that destroys animals' homes, and scientific experiments are a few of the things that have caused unnecessary suffering to animals and have endangered the existence of many species. Do you think animals are entitled to a bill of rights? What do you think the consequences of such a bill might be? Would you join the group?

Write a letter to the animal rights group stating your position about a Bill of Rights for Animals. Begin your letter with "Dear Members:" and tell them whether or not you will join them. Explain what you agree with or disagree with. Since your response could seriously affect the action this group takes, you want your position to be fully supported by logical reasoning and good examples.

Dear Members:

Although I believe your draft for a Bill of Rights for Animals could be a good thing, I have many questions about joining and do not feel I can support everything you say. I agree that animals should be given protection so that they're not killed by barrages of hunters for fun and recreation or driven out of their natural habitat by developers, but scientific experiments must be allowed to go on.

Hunting laws should be more strictly enforced. We have to keep a balance in nature going. Certain birds, animals, and fish have almost disappeared because of human greed. Whales and dolphin need international protection. Hunting for furs has endangered whole species like leopards and tigers and even many American animals like beavers and fox. Yet we still have to have food and many of the products that come from animals, so I am not totally against killing or hunting animals. I just feel that the laws have to be fair and strictly enforced to keep the balance of nature.

I do feel strongly against unnecessary land development that really upsets the balance of nature. Not only are animals displaced, but trees and open space are destroyed. There used to be a forest at the top of the hill where I live, and now it is a ten-story high rise apartment house. When I used to go there a while ago, I often saw a family of deer. It makes me mad to think of the wild life that's gone from up there especially when I always see so many older apartment houses up for sale.

The thing I question most about your Bill of Rights, however, is your objection to the use of animals for research. You say that scientific experiments are endangering the lives of animals, but, many diseases which used to endanger human lives have been cured with the help of laboratory animals which are used for this purpose. I would be against the bill if it called for no testing of animals because scientists searching for new information to help society wouldn't be able to use them.

I admire what you are doing, but I'm afraid that an Animal Bill of Rights would stop a lot of good work as well as some of the bad things. Why not just work with other environmentalists to get some strong laws passed that would make the earth a better and safer place to live for all the animals, including the human ones?

Sincerely,
Jane Murray

Paper G

Score $\boxed{6}$

Notes	Discussion Prompts
Content/Organization	

Notes	Discussion Prompts
1. This is a serious consideration of the topic in which the writer thoughtfully weighs her ideas. The letter is well organized, with a beginning that sets up the argument, a middle section that focuses on each issue, and a logical conclusion that has grown out of the argument.	1. Is this paper well organized? Give three reasons why you think it is.
2. Ideas are presented in a logical sequence, making it easy for the reader to follow.	2. Are the ideas logically presented? Use one paragraph to illustrate.
3. Details and examples illustrate the points being made.	3. How does the writer illustrate her points?
4. Good transitional devices and careful repetition help the reader.	4. How does the writer link ideas?
5. Paragraphs are unified and coherent. Each one has a central idea, which is developed by sentences that clearly connect one part of the idea to the next.	5. What is the central idea in each paragraph? Are there any sentences that do not support the main ideas?

Sentence Construction	
1. The writer demonstrates knowledge of how to combine ideas into interesting and mature statements.	1. Find at least three examples of sentences in which several ideas have been correctly tied together. Explain how the writer did it.
2. There is a good variety of sentences, from simple to complex.	2. Does the writer give us a variety of sentence constructions? Is this important? Why?

Usage	
1. Unclear and indefinite pronoun references (par. 3) can confuse the reader.	1. Do you find any vagueness in paragraph 3? Where does an idea lose focus? How would you correct this?
2. Word choice is excellent. Although the occasion is a formal one, the writer's voice is natural, correct, and sincere.	2. Who is the audience for this letter and what is the purpose of it? Do you think the language is accurate and effective? Give examples.

Mechanics	
1. The writer has a good command of the mechanics of spelling, punctuation, and capitalization, and only uses one unnecessary comma.	1. Proofread the paper to see if there are any errors in spelling or punctuation.

Prompt #5: Animal Rights

An animal rights group has asked you to join them to draft a Bill of Rights for Animals. The group believes that hunting rights, new land development that destroys animals' homes, and scientific experiments are a few of the things that have caused unnecessary suffering to animals and have endangered the existence of many species. Do you think animals are entitled to a bill of rights? What do you think the consequences of such a bill might be? Would you join the group?

Write a letter to the animal rights group stating your position about a Bill of Rights for Animals. Begin your letter with "Dear Members:" and tell them whether or not you will join them. Explain what you agree with or disagree with. Since your response could seriously affect the action this group takes, you want your position to be fully supported by logical reasoning and good examples.

Dear Members,

I will not join you on account of that I go hunting and, I cant support you. The Destruction of animals homes is not right but scientific work is O.K. because it gives us answers. Dont think that I'm cruel to animals. Animals have rights, I know they do but, if you stop land developement you will take away someone's job. As far as the hunting, people have been hunting since Mankind and it didnt bother, so why should they stop it. Its legal isnt it? and thats why I dont think they should make a bill of rights for animals. And the consequences if the Bill goes into effect. Scientists might have to experiment on people, workers might loss their jobs, hunters would stop enjoying their sport. I know people think that hunting is a Savage sport but its not. They wouldnt make it legal if it was.

Yours,
Walter Fox

Paper H

Score 2

Notes	Discussion Prompts
Content/Organization	
1. The writer does not know how to paragraph ideas and develop them.	1. How many different paragraphs could you write based on this paper? What facts, reasons, or ideas would you use to develop them?
2. The paper lacks organization. Although it has a beginning statement, sentences in the middle attempt to answer the question as if it were a test instead of an essay.	2. Once you have a list of paragraph topics, how would you organize them?
3. There is no conclusion; the paper just stops with the writer's support of hunting.	3. Does the essay have a satisfying conclusion? What would you add or change?
Sentence Construction	
1. The writer uses run-ons and fragments.	1. Locate and correct all run-on sentences and fragments.
2. An incorrect conjunction (sent. 1) joins two ideas in a sentence.	2. Find better connecting words between clauses in the first sentence.
Usage	
1. A general carelessness, or perhaps haste in working out ideas, makes the writer omit words or choose the wrong word.	1. The writer sometimes omits important connecting words. Reread the paper to find places where filling in missing words would make the meaning clear.
2. Vague pronoun references cause confusion.	2. *It* and *they* are often misused as pronouns when they don't refer to specific antecedents. Find examples of that error in this paper.
3. Homonym errors occur.	3. Check the paper for homonym errors.
Mechanics	
1. There are many punctuation errors involving commas and apostrophes. A colon should be used in a formal salutation.	1. Proofread the paper for all punctuation errors.
2. There are capitalization errors.	2. Has the writer used capital letters correctly?
3. There are two spelling errors	3. Proofread for spelling errors.

Prompt #6: Moral Dilemma

One of your closest friends has asked you to help him (or her) convince his parents that he was at your house when, in fact, he was at a party with other friends of whom his parents disapprove. Your friend is afraid his (or her) parents will punish him severely if they find out. Now you have a problem you must solve—how best to help your friend. Although you value the friendship, you are uncomfortable about what you have been asked to do, but you would like to be able to help your friend.

Write a letter telling your friend whether or not you have decided to help him (or her). In either case, support your decision with good reasons for your action and suggest a way to solve the problem that will improve your friend's relationship with his parents and not endanger your friendship with him.

Dear Stacy:

Did you enjoy that party at your "cool" friends' house? Did you really honestly think that this party was worth lying to your one and only parent's? Because I am really your friend, I have decided not to go along with you on this. I cannot lie to your parent's. They are kind, trusting, and care about you. They trust you and me, to tell them the truth when they ask for it, and I think they deserve it.

You made a mistake in telling them, that you were going to be at my house. Didn't you realize you were putting me in trouble! If they were to find out the truth, they would never trust me again either, and they would never treat me the same. Right now I can come and go in your house just as you can in mine. Even our parent's are good friends. Can you imagine what would happen if my parent's found out that I had lied for you?

I don't think that if I were to ask you to do the same thing for me, you wouldn't be eager to do it. What you are doing and asking me to do is telling a lie. You know how much I despise liars, and now you're asking me to become one!

Stacy, your parent's treat you with respect and honesty. They expect you to treat them with the same kind of respect and honesty. You can't see this, but they are trying to treat you like an adult, instead of a kid. I think you should start acting like one, if you want them to keep treating you as an adult. Your parent's deserve the truth, not from someone else, but from you.

Sally

Paper M

Notes	Discussion Prompts
Content/Organization	
1. The writer has a good sense of organization. The opening paragraph sets the tone, focuses on the major argument, and attracts interest. The last paragraph is a strongly stated conclusion logically based on what has been written.	1. List three things you've noticed about the way this paper is organized.
2. The writer uses paragraphs for each new idea.	2. Is there a topic sentence in each paragraph?
3. Some ideas need more development. The writer makes bold statements but doesn't always develop them with examples.	3. Are there any ideas that need further development?
Sentence Construction	
1. The writer uses a variety of sentence forms and structures effectively.	1. Does the writer use a variety of sentences? Are the sentences effective and appropriate?
2. Two sentences would improve with parallel structure (par. 1, sent. 2; par. 3, sent. 1).	2. Can you find any sentences that would improve with parallel structure?
3. In the next-to-last sentence of the last paragraph, the dependent clause belongs at the beginning of the sentence.	3. Look at the next-to-last sentence in the last paragraph. What's the main point of that sentence? Does the sentence construction achieve it? Explain.
Usage	
1. A double negative (par. 3, sent. 1) confuses the reader.	1. The opening sentence of paragraph 3 is confusing. Why? How would you change it to clarify the writer's meaning?
2. The language is serious but friendly. The reader believes the writer's sincerity.	2. How would you describe the author's vocabulary and use of language? Do you think it's appropriate and effective in terms of the writer's audience and purpose?
Mechanics	
1. The writer consistently misspells a key word in the letter. (The student is referring to Stacy's *parents*, the plural, not the possessive.)	1. Which word is misspelled and why is that an important error?
2. Although the writer often uses commas correctly, there are two places where commas are unnecessary (par. 1, last sent.; par. 2, sent. 1).	2. Edit for punctuation and correct the errors wherever you find them.

Prompt #6: Moral Dilemma

One of your closest friends has asked you to help him (or her) convince his parents that he was at your house when, in fact, he was at a party with other friends of whom his parents disapprove. Your friend is afraid his (or her) parents will punish him severely if they find out. Now you have a problem you must solve—how best to help your friend. Although you value the friendship, you are uncomfortable about what you have been asked to do, but you would like to be able to help your friend.

Write a letter telling your friend whether or not you have decided to help him (or her). In either case, support your decision with good reasons for your action and suggest a way to solve the problem that will improve your friend's relationship with his parents and not endanger your friendship with him.

To Chuck:

No, I will not lie to your parents.

My reason is one day you and your friends might go to a party where the people are using drugs. If the peer presure rises you will probly take some drugs to.

I dont want to explain to your parents why you become a drug user.

Even if that doesn't happen I still dont want to get involved. Maybe next time I'll be away and wont be able to lie for you.

You shouldn't have went to the party. So if I went to a party that I wasnt suppose to go to. I wouldn't ask you to lie to my parents.

Why dont you talk to your parents, dont tell them you went to the party yet.

But maybe if your parents met these people she will like them alot more. And by that time your parents will forget about the party.

And while your at it show your parents all the good grades you get in school.

And all the bad ones tell them you'll bring the grades up next time.

And if your parents dont like them ask them there reasons and if its that bad maybe they shouldn't really be your friends.

Paper P

Score | 1 |

Notes	Discussion Prompts
Content/Organization	
1. The writer doesn't know how to organize ideas into paragraphs and to develop them with reasons and examples. There are one-line ideas that need to be connected to similar ideas and developed into coherent statements.	1. How would you help this writer organize these ideas into paragraphs? What is the first piece of advice you would give the writer?
2. The content is immature. The writer either hasn't given the situation much thought or is just giving poor advice.	2. What is your response to the content? What questions would you ask the writer?
3. The letter needs a conclusion based on the argument.	3. Are you satisfied with the ending? Given the ideas this writer has, what would be a logical conclusion?
4. The salutation and complimentary closing are missing, but this is not inappropriate in a friendly letter.	4. Is the letter form appropriate?
Sentence Construction	
1. The writer uses run-on sentences and fragments.	1. Edit for run-on sentences and fragments.
2. Writers should avoid beginning sentences with conjunctions. They read like fragments.	2. What's wrong with beginning a sentence with a conjunction like *and, but,* or *so*? What effect do these sentences have on the reader?
3. Short, choppy sentences should be combined into longer sentences to show the relationship between ideas.	3. Do you see any ideas that could be combined into stronger sentences?
4. Missing conjunctions, phrases, and even sentences to connect ideas make the ideas difficult to follow.	4. Where did you find it difficult to understand the logical connection between ideas? What conjunctions would you use? What sentences or phrases would you add to connect ideas?
5. Incorrect verb tense interferes with meaning.	5. Edit for correct verb tense.
Usage	
1. Vague and faulty pronoun references interfere with understanding.	1. Examine the use of pronouns. Are they correct and clear? Change any that are not.
2. There are homonym errors.	2. Proofread for mistakes in homonyms.
Mechanics	
1. Punctuation problems with apostrophes and commas occur.	1. Edit for punctuation. Explain your decisions.
2. There are three spelling errors.	2. Proofread for spelling errors.